MAN IN THE NEW TESTAMENT

MAN IN THE
NEW TESTAMENT

by

WERNER GEORG KÜMMEL

*Professor of New Testament in
the University of Marburg*

Translated by

JOHN J. VINCENT

Revised and enlarged edition

THE WESTMINSTER PRESS:
PHILADELPHIA

© THE EPWORTH PRESS 1963

Library of Congress Catalog Card No. 63–10420

The first edition of
MAN IN THE NEW TESTAMENT
was published in 1948 by Zwingli-Verlag, Zürich, as
Das Bild des Menschen im Neuen Testament.

PRINTED AND BOUND IN ENGLAND BY
HAZELL WATSON AND VINEY LTD
AYLESBURY AND SLOUGH

Contents

Foreword

When some of my English friends and fellow-workers in New Testament studies most generously suggested that my book, *Das Bild des Menschen im Neuen Testament*, might be translated into English, I cordially concurred. However, it was impossible simply to republish a book which first appeared in 1948, especially one concerning a subject upon which so much debate has taken place over the last ten years. At the same time, I had not the time, because of other commitments, to rewrite the whole volume.

It seemed best, therefore, to leave the text unaltered, but considerably to enlarge the footnotes to take note of the present state of studies on the problem. This solution seemed good also, inasmuch as I hold that the statement of the matter as it stands in the first edition is still valid, and I would not wish to alter it. It was necessary only to deal with certain single points in greater detail, and to indicate the foundation for them in a more comprehensive way. In well over half of the footnotes, therefore, additions have been made, although the old footnote numbers have been retained. The eight entirely new footnotes are numbered '6a', etc. I hope that this will also assist those who have used the book in its German edition (which is at present out of print). They can readily see by reference to the footnotes the ways in which I now either elaborate my position or take issue with other scholars.

The lively discussion with British theologians which followed a lecture on part of the subject of this book, which I was privileged to give to the Society for the Study of Theology at Nottingham during Easter 1961, indicated the great interest which the Christian Doctrine of Man has today, and encouraged me to hope that a helpful debate will follow the appearance of this book in the English-speaking world.

I should like to express my hearty thanks to the Reverend Dr John J. Vincent for the kind service he has done in translating so sympathetically and accurately not merely the words but also the ideas I wish to express.

WERNER GEORG KÜMMEL

Marburg/Lahn
8 April 1961

Abbreviations

ETh   *Evangelische Theologie*
ExpT   *Expository Times*
JBL   *Journal of Biblical Literature*
LThK   *Lexikon für Theologie und Kirche* (2nd edn)
NTSt   *New Testament Studies*
RGG   *Die Religion in Geschichte und Gegenwart*
ThBl   *Theologische Blätter*
ThLZ   *Theologische Literaturzeitung*
ThR   *Theologische Rundschau*
ThT   *Theology Today*
ThWb   *Theologisches Wörterbuch zum Neuen Testament*, ed. G. Kittel and G. Friedrich
ThZ   *Theologische Zeitschrift*
ZNW   *Zeitschrift für die Neutestamentliche Wissenschaft und die Kunde der älteren Kirche*
ZThK   *Zeitschrift für Theologie und Kirche*

Bultmann, *G.u.V.*   Rudolf Bultmann, *Glauben und Verstehen*, I (1933), II–III (1952–60).

Bultmann, *Geschichte.* Rudolf Bultmann, *Die Geschichte der synoptischen Tradition*, 2nd edn (1931) (= 3rd edn, 1958 with Supplement).

Bultmann, *Theology*.   Rudolf Bultmann, *Theology of the New Testament*, I (1952), II (1955). (Eng. tr. of *Theologie des Neuen Testaments*, 2nd edn, 1950.) Ger. 3rd edn (1958).

Kümmel, *Bekehrung*.   W. G. Kümmel, *Römer 7 und die Bekehrung des Paulus* (1929).

Kümmel, *Promise*.   W. G. Kümmel, *Promise and Fulfilment* (1957). (Eng. tr. of *Verheissung und Erfüllung*, 3rd edn, 1956.)

NEB   *New English Bible* (1961).

ONE

The Problem

WHAT DOES the New Testament have to say
about Man—the Man to whom the Christian
message is addressed? The question has for a long
time been one of the chief preoccupations of systematic theological thought. Several detailed studies
of theological anthropology have appeared in recent
years.[1]

For this reason, it is the more surprising that
New Testament studies have not for a considerable
period directed any detailed attention to this prob-

[1] T. Haecker, *Was ist der Mensch?* (1933); Edmund Schlink,
Der Mensch in der Verkündigung der Kirche (1936); Emil Brunner,
*Der Mensch im Widerspruch. Die christliche Lehre vom wirklichen
und vom wahren Menschen* (1937) (ET, *Man in Revolt*, 1947);
W. Bachmann, *Gottes Ebenbild. Ein systematischer Versuch einer
christlichen Lehre vom Menschen* (1938); Reinhold Niebuhr, *The
Nature and Destiny of Man*, I and II (1941 and 1943); Helmut
Thielicke, *Tod und Leben. Studien zur christlichen Anthropologie*
(1946); Karl Barth, *Die kirchliche Dogmatik*, III, part 2 (1948)
(ET, *Church Dogmatics*, III.2 [1960]); W. Trillhaas, *Vom Wesen
des Menschen* (1949); Friedrich Gogarten, *Der Mensch zwischen
Gott und Welt* (1952); H. Thielicke, *Theologische Ethik*, II,
part 1 (1955), pp. 328ff.

On more recent anthropological studies in English, cf. H. T.
Kerr, 'The Human Problem in Contemporary Thought', *ThT*,
I.(1944).158ff. Further literature references are given in the
articles '*Anthropologie, IV, Dogmatisch*', by Regin Prenter, in
RGG, I.(3rd edn, 1957).423–4, and '*Anthropologie, Theologische*',
by K. Rahner, in *LThK*, I.(1957).627.

lem. Franz Delitzsch was the last to give an overall picture of the biblical view of man, a hundred years ago, in his *System der biblischen Psychologie* (2nd edn, 1861). This book, however, is completely out of date, since it proceeds from the assumption of the 'undeniably uniform character of the psychological material present in the scriptures' (p. 15), and consequently puts everything on the same plane. Apart from this, Delitzsch poses many questions to the text which it cannot possibly answer, and then offers quite fantastic theosophical theories as interpretation of it.

In the last half-century, so far as I know, only two works on New Testament Psychology have appeared.[2] Both books are primarily concerned with the attempt to define the 'psychological terms' of the New Testament. Such an attempt is, however, hopeless. We simply cannot say what the occasional anthropological terms of the New Testament meant in relation one to another. Again, both these books completely omit any consideration of the New Testament view of man as a whole. E. de Witt Burton[3] has discussed anthropological terminology within the framework of general religious history. His work is very valuable as a collection of background material. It was not his intention, however, to give the complete New Testament view of

[2] M. Scott Fletcher, *The Psychology of the New Testament* (1912); M. Wohlrab, *Grundriss der neutestamentlichen Psychologie* (1913). I have been unable to consult E. H. van Leeuwen, *Bijbelsche Anthropologie* (1906).

[3] *Spirit, Soul and Flesh* (1918).

man. Since then a few specialized works on isolated anthropological concepts have appeared,[4] and a few short surveys.[5]

[4] Adolf Schlatter, *'Herz und Gehirn im ersten Jahrhundert'*, *Studien zur systematischen Theologie, Th. von Haering . . . dargebracht* (1918), pp. 86ff; E. von Dobschütz, *'Die fünf Sinne im Neuen Testament'*, *JBL*, XLVIII.(1929).378ff; C. Guignebert, *'Remarques sur quelques conceptions chrétiennes antiques, touchant l'origine et la nature de l'âme'*, *Rev. d'histoire et de philosophie religieuses* (1929), pp. 428ff; O. Moe, *'Vernunft und Geist im Neuen Testament'*, *Zeitschrift für Syst. Theol.*, XI.(1934).351ff; Eduard Schweizer, *'Die hellenistische Komponente im neutestamentlichen sarx-Begriff'*, *ZNW*, XLVIII.(1957).237ff; K. G. Kuhn, 'New Light on Temptation, Sin and Flesh in the New Testament', in *The Scrolls and the New Testament*, ed. K. Stendahl (1957), pp. 94ff.

From the *Theologisches Wörterbuch zum Neuen Testament* (up to Vol. VII, p. 160) the articles which are most relevant are: *'Anthropos'* (J. Jeremias), I.365ff; *'Thanatos'* (R. Bultmann), III.7ff; *'Nous'* (J. Behm), IV.950ff; *'Pneuma'* (E. Schweizer), VI.394ff; *'Sarx'* (E. Schweizer), VII.123ff.

[5] J. M. Nielen, *'Der Mensch in der Verkündigung des Evangeliums'*, in *Das Bild vom Menschen: Beiträge zur theologischen und philosophischen Anthropologie, F. Tillmann zum 60. Geburtstag* (1934), pp. 14ff; K. Th. Schaefer, *'Der Mensch in paulinischer Auffassung'*, ibid. pp. 25ff; H. Schlier, *'Vom Menschenbild des Neuen Testaments'*, in *Der alte und der neue Mensch; Beiträge zur Evangelischen Theologie*, VIII.(1942).24ff; O. A. Piper, 'The Biblical Understanding of Man', *ThT*, I.(1944).188ff; K. Galling, *Das Bild vom Menschen in biblischer Sicht* (Mainzer Universitäts-Reden 3, 1947); C. H. Dodd, P. I. Bratsiosis, R. Bultmann, H. Clavier, *Man in God's Design according to the New Testament* (1952); Rudolph Bultmann, *'Das Verständnis von Welt und Mensch im Neuen Testament und im Griechentum'*, *G.u.V.*, II.(1952).59ff; R. Bultmann, *'Adam, wo bist du? Ueber das Menschenbild der Bibel'*, *G.u.V.*, II.(1952).105ff; H. D. Wendland, *'Vom Menschenbild des Neuen Testaments'*, *Dienst unter dem Wort. Festschrift für H. Schreiner* (1933), pp. 306ff; J. N. Sevenster, *'Die Anthropologie des Neuen Testaments'*,

Now, an examination of particular anthropological concepts is certainly indispensable. But the biblical-theological view of the New Testament understanding of man is something much more all-embracing. Biblical theology needs to have a clear picture of man as depicted or presupposed in the New Testament, primarily because such a picture necessarily lies behind the proclamation of God's saving acts directed towards man. Only through an insight into this basic conception of man can the New Testament message of salvation really be made comprehensible.

Up till now, this important task has only been taken in hand seriously in the area of Pauline anthropology.[6] Paul, of course, offers the most

Supplements to *Numen*, II.(1955).166ff; J. Schmid, art. '*Anthropologie, Biblische*', *LThK*, I.(1957).604ff; E. Fuchs, *Zum hermeneutischen Problem in der Theologie* (1959), pp. 154ff: 'Prolegomena to a lecture on the anthropology of the NT'; and 261ff: 'The Biblical View of Man'; N. A. Dahl, art. '*Mensch, II: im NT*', in *RGG*, IV.(3rd edn, 1960).863ff; R. Bultmann, '*Der Mensch und seine Welt nach dem Urteil der Bibel*', *G.u.V.*, III.(1960).151ff.

[6] W. Schauf, *Sarx. Der Begriff Fleisch beim Apostel Paulus unter besonderer Berücksichtigung seiner Erlösungslehre* (1924); W. G. Kümmel, *Bekehrung*, pp. 14ff; W. Gutbrod, *Die paulinische Anthropologie* (1934); P. Althaus, *Paulus und Luther über den Menschen* (2nd edn, 1951); H. Mehl-Koehnlein, *L'homme selon l'apôtre Paul* (1951); J. A. T. Robinson, *The Body. A Study in Pauline Anthropology* (1952); W. D. Stacey, *The Pauline View of Man, in relation to its Judaic and Hellenistic Background* (1956); W. D. Davies, 'Paul and the Dead Sea Scrolls: Flesh and Spirit', in *The Scrolls* . . . (note 4, *supra*), pp. 157ff; W. Matthias, '*Der alte und der neue Mensch in der Anthropologie des Paulus*', *ETh*, XVII.(1957).385ff; R. P. Shedd, *Man in Community*.

relevant material. But Paul's message is only one part of the New Testament, and presents so many unsolved problems precisely in its anthropology that we must place it alongside the anthropological statements of the rest of the New Testament. In this way, we shall discover both its distinctive sense and also its meaning within the New Testament as a whole.

If this is a correct summary of the present situation regarding this question, then it will be plain that a fresh examination of the New Testament concept of man is appropriate. Rather than offering an exhaustive picture, we shall set out as clearly as possible the witness of the three most important forms of the New Testament message: the preaching of Jesus in the synoptic kerygma, the teaching of Paul, and the theology of John. We shall then compare the statements of the remaining New Testament writings with these three main forms.

One further limitation of our task is unavoidable. The New Testament is only interested in man in relation to God. All Christological, theological, cosmological and ethical statements only serve to

A Study of St Paul's Application of Old Testament and Early Jewish Conceptions of Human Solidarity (1958); S. Laeuchli, 'Monism and Dualism in the Pauline Anthropology', Biblical Research, III.(1958).15ff; R. Bultmann, Theology, I.227–59 (Ger. 191ff); O. Kuss, Der Römerbrief, Part II (1959), pp. 506ff; W. R. Nelson, 'Pauline Anthropology. Its Relation to Christ and His Church', Interpretation, XIV.(1960).14ff. E. Rissanen, 'Züge aus der Anthropologie des Paulus', Theologia Fennica, III. (1943).28ff, is an all too short abstract, which does not bring anything new forward.

describe God's manward act of salvation and to urge mankind to a right response. Because of this the New Testament message provides not only a picture of the man to whom the message is addressed, but also a description of the *renewed* mankind which results from God's action. Hence it would be perfectly justifiable to include in our study all statements about the nature of the *Christian* man, as has already been done many times. That would be, however, to go beyond the New Testament concept of man as such.

Moreover, it would be to open wider questions relating to the nature and intention of the divine act of salvation, the whole concept of the new creation, and the moral implications of the Christian life. All this would take us too far, and we must confine ourselves to asking the basic question: 'How does the New Testament see the man to whom the message of Jesus Christ comes?' [6a] If we can find

[6a] Karl Barth's thesis in *Christus und Adam nach Römer*, V. (1952).10–11, 50, 52, that 'already our former existence outside Christ . . . was a real existence, even if hidden, in Him', that Jesus Christ is 'the Secret and the Truth of human nature as such', turns the New Testament picture of man upside-down. It is indeed true that we can only understand the human from the Christian, but it is quite false to suggest that 'we are already simply as men . . . inside the Kingdom of Christ'. Romans 5^{12-21} speaks not of Christ as 'the real man', but of the universality of death in Adam, and the universal possibility of life in Christ. (Cf. on this point, R. Bultmann, '*Adam und Christus nach Röm 5*', *ZNW*, L.[1959].145ff.) Again, it is not correct that man as such 'is the creature whose Kinsman (*Artgenosse*), Neighbour and Brother this man Jesus is' (*Kirchl. Dogm.*, III.2 *passim*, esp. pp. 158ff; *Church Dogm.*, III.2 *passim*, esp. pp.

the answer to this question, we can also conclude what kind of salvation it must be which will save such a man, and also how he can lay hold of it.

160ff) if one is talking about the man to whom the message of Christ first comes—that is, to man *before* faith. (Cf. here E. Brunner, '*Der neue Barth*', *ZThK*, XLVIII.[1951].97ff.) In both cases, the uniqueness of the incarnation of Jesus is lost, together with the uniqueness of the *alteration* of man's historical situation first made possible in it. These saving facts are lost in favour of an *idea* of a true man mirrored in the reality of man as he exists.

TWO

Jesus in the Synoptic Kerygma

JESUS PROCLAIMED the imminence of the
Kingdom of God, which was already breaking
through in His own person,[7] and which demanded
of man repentance (*metanoia*), forcing every man
to decision in the face of this approach of God's
kingdom bringing with it judgement and division.[8] This is clear from the saying of Mark 1^{15}:
'The time is fulfilled and the Kingdom of God is at
hand, repent and believe in the Gospel', although
in its present form this is the construction of the
early Church. But it is clear also from the several
genuine sayings of Jesus which make *metanoia* the
essential pre-condition for withstanding the judgement of God or for entering into God's Kingdom
(Mt 11^{21-2}, 12^{41}). This call for *metanoia* is central
both in the message of the prophets and also in
later Judaism. Its main object is not in the first
place to awaken a feeling of guilt, although this is
naturally not excluded (Mt 11^{21}, Lk 7^{37-8}). Its primary content is the demand that man should turn
aside from the wrong way and embark upon the way
which is the will of God (cf. especially the parable
of the Prodigal Son: Luke 15^{11-12}, and also Luke 9^{62}).

[7] For the evidence for this, see my *Promise and Fulfilment*.
[8] Cf. my brief remarks in *Judaica*, I.(1945).60–1.

In Jesus, this call to conversion is now clearly directed towards *all* mankind. This is clear, not only from the fact that all are asked to respond to the call to repent, but also, and principally, from the warning of Jesus to His listeners that they, like the Galileans killed by Pilate, or those upon whom the tower of Siloam fell, would be destroyed if they did not repent (Lk 15^{1ff}). Man must learn that all he can do is call upon the grace of God, as the publican does (Lk 18^{9ff}). Moreover, if this call to repentance is directed to all men, it must be presumed that all men *need* such a conversion; and from that it can be concluded that the prevalence of sin in all men is, for Jesus, a self-evident element in His view of man, even if it is not dogmatically formulated.

Two objections can be offered to this statement. (1) On the one hand, it can be pointed out that Jesus expressly said that He had not come to call the righteous, but sinners (Mk 2^{17b}), and that in the conclusion of the parable of the lost sheep, He contrasts the ninety-nine righteous who have no need for repentance with the one sinner who does repent (Lk 15^7). From these two texts some have wanted to deduce that Jesus presumed the existence of those who were righteous.[9] This deduction, however, is certainly wrong. The saying, 'I came not to call the righteous, but sinners' (Mk 2^{17b}),

[9] H. J. Holtzmann, *Lehrbuch der Neutestamentlichen Theologie*, I.(2nd edn, 1911).218-19; Adolf Jülicher, *Die Gleichnisreden Jesu*, II.(1910).323.

which is added to the pericope about intercourse
with publicans, is scarcely a secondary conclusion
to an early Christian sermon, as some suggest.[10]
Rather, it is the pointed and striking answer of
Jesus Himself to the criticism that He is a 'Friend
of publicans and sinners'.[11]

Now the discrimination made here between the
righteous and the sinners, which Jesus takes over
from the words of His opponents, is certainly not
intended ironically, as Jesus recognized throughout
a relative distinction between the righteous and
sinners (Mt 5[45], 13[49], 25[37, 46]). Jesus is not concerned here with whether there are such people as
the righteous (*dikaioi*). Rather it is His intention to
tell His opponents who see themselves as righteous
rather than as sinful, that His call to salvation is
directed precisely at those who are ready to listen
to Him because they are aware of their sinfulness.
His opponents' mistake lies in the fact that they
exclude themselves from insight into their own
sinfulness, whereas Jesus presupposes that all

[10] So R. Bultmann, *Geschichte*, p. 96, and Supplement, p. 14;
M. Dibelius, *Formgeschichte des Evangeliums* (2nd edn, 1933)
(= 3rd edn, 1959), pp. 60–1 (ET, *From Tradition to Gospel*
[1935], p. 64); C. H. Dodd, *The Parables of the Kingdom* (3rd
edn, 1936), p. 118.

[11] So rightly J. Sundwall, '*Die Zusammensetzung des Markus-
evangeliums*', *Acta Academiae Aboensis, Humaniora*, IX.2.(1934).
15–16 (who wishes to exclude Mark 2[17a] as an addition); Vincent
Taylor, *The Gospel According to St Mark* (1952), p. 207; A.
Descamps, *Les Justes et la Justice dans les évangiles et le christianisme
primitif hormis la doctrine proprement paulinienne* (1950), pp. 108–9.
Cf. also W. G. Kümmel, *ZNW*, XXXIII.(1934). 120, note 56.

men, including these 'righteous ones', are sinful.

It is the same in Luke 15[7]. In the conclusion of the parable of the lost sheep, there seems to be a clear implication that among a hundred men there are ninety-nine who need no repentance. Here, too, we are not dealing with a secondary application.[12] What is being said in subtle form is that God expects conversion from all sinners. The question of whether there are, beside the sinners, also men who are righteous—either few or many—is not even asked. In Luke 18[14a], however, it is clearly shown that Jesus by such a paradoxical expression intended to make the critics see that they also must consider themselves as sinners. Here the Pharisee who feels himself righteous before God is in the wrong, and the tax-collector who recognizes his guilt before God is shown to be right. The same thing is found in the rule about not taking the chief seats at a marriage feast (Lk 14[8-10]), which was originally a parable exhorting man to be aware of his lowliness and unworthiness in view of the forthcoming judgement.[13]

It is therefore clear that Jesus does not want to

[12] So R. Bultmann, *Geschichte*, p. 184.

[13] For this understanding of the text, cf. M. Dibelius (note 10 *supra*), p. 116, note 1, and pp. 248-9 (ET, pp. 119, 248); similarly, B. T. D. Smith, *The Parables of the Synoptic Gospels* (1937), pp. 207-8. The word '*Parabole*' is consequently hardly to be translated as 'rule', as J. Jeremias thinks: *Die Gleichnisse Jesu* (4th edn. 1956), pp. 14, 162 (ET, *The Parables of Jesus* [1954], pp. 18, 135).

obviate the moral difference between 'good' and
'bad', but desires that precisely those who think
themselves blameless in God's sight shall understand their guilt before God.[14] It is consistent with
this that Jesus commonly speaks to His listeners in
general as 'evil' (*poneroi*) (Mt 7[11] par. Lk 11[13])
and calls His contemporaries an 'adulterous and
sinful generation' (Mk 8[38], Mt 12[39], 16[4]). The argument that Jesus recognizes the existence of righteous as well as sinners is therefore not tenable.

(2) The second argument against our statement
that Jesus presupposes the common sinfulness of
all mankind is a more serious one. A. von Harnack
has, as is well known, maintained in his lectures on
The Essence of Christianity that in the text 'For
what shall it profit a man, if he shall gain the whole
world and lose his own soul?' (Mk 8[36], Luther and
AV) Jesus puts the highest possible value on man's
natural worth. 'He who can say "Father" to the
Being who rules Heaven and Earth, is raised above
Heaven and Earth and has himself a value that is
higher than the structure of the world.'[15] If that

[14] Cf. also G. Schrenk, *ThWb*, II.191–2, and W. Grundmann,
ThWb, I.306, note 138.

[15] A. von Harnack, *Das Wesen des Christentums* (4th edn, 1901),
pp. 43–4. In *Lehrbuch der Dogmengeschichte* I.(4th edn, 1909).
80, Harnack speaks of 'The thought of the inestimable value
which each individual soul possesses by its own right.' Further, H. J. Holtzmann (note 9, *supra*) I.(2nd edn, 1911).230;
H. Weinel, *RGG*, III.(2nd edn, 1929).167; W. Jaeger, *Paideia*,
II.(2nd edn, 1954).90 (ET, II.[1944].41). Also P. I. Bratsiotis
(note 5, *supra*) finds here expressed 'the weighty superiority of
the soul over the body'.

were right, one would have to conclude that Jesus
could scarcely have maintained the common sinfulness and need for salvation of all mankind; for if
man has an infinite value in God's eyes, he cannot
face God as being completely reliant on His forgiveness and succour.

However, it is far from clear what was the original meaning of the two texts Mark 8[35 and 36], which
probably did not originally belong together. We
must consider them in a little more detail.

'Whosoever will save his life shall lose it;
   But whosoever shall lose his life for my sake
      and the Gospel's, the same shall save it.
   For what shall it profit a man, if he shall gain
      the whole world, and lose his life?'

According to one widely held interpretation, what
we have here are two secular sayings concerning
the incomparable value of man's earthly life, which,
by being introduced into the context of the Gospel,
have received a completely different meaning by
being connected with the winning of eternal life.[16]
But the suggestion that secular wisdom-sayings
have been taken over here is not at all certain.
Moreover, when one recalls that '*psuche*' in these

[16] So particularly R. Bultmann, *Geschichte*, pp. 86, 101–2, 107.
A more cautious view, positing a new interpretation given to the
words by Jesus, is urged by K. L. Schmidt, *RGG*, III.(2nd edn,
1929).133, and Julius Schniewind, *Das Evangelium nach Markus*
(1933), pp. 113–14.

texts corresponds to the Jewish concept of 'life', it becomes much more probable that Mark 8[35], by using from the outset the double meaning of 'life' (earthly and heavenly life), emphasizes the necessity of renouncing the earthly life to win the heavenly, and that 8[36] shows up the worthlessness of earthly acquisitions in comparison with the loss of heavenly life.[17] And so these texts just do not take for granted the special value of the human soul: on the contrary, they are intended to warn man about the danger of losing eternal life.

However, one cannot simply, by explaining the text in this way, dismiss from it the whole question of whether Jesus has attributed such a high value to the soul of man as Harnack maintained. One must further ask whether the assertion that Jesus sees man as a sinner before God is confirmed by other relevant sayings of Jesus.

If Jesus sees man as a sinner, then it might be said that He sees man basically not from any human standpoint but only from God's point of view. This is not, however, self-evident. For whether, in the mind of Jesus, man has a value in himself as an individual, and how man is so looked at in detail, depend precisely upon the *role* played by man's place before God in the thinking of Jesus.

[17] See E. de Witt Burton (note 3, *supra*), p. 184; E. Klostermann, *Das Markusevangelium* (3rd edn, 1936), pp. 84–5; F. Hauck, *Das Evangelium des Markus* (1931), pp. 105–6; A. Stumpff, *ThWb*, III.893–4; V. Taylor, *Mark*, p. 382; J. N. Sevenster (note 5, *supra*), p. 174; J. Schmid (note 5, *supra*), p. 610.

Now Jesus proclaimed the nearness of *God's* Kingdom and, in face of this pressing eschatological
situation, demanded from man conversion and
obedience towards the newly proclaimed will of
God. With this preaching of the coming of God's
Kingdom, Jesus was using a current, lively, Jewish
eschatological expectation, which, however, only
seldom made use of an unequivocally future idea
of the Kingdom of God.[18] It is thus very note-
worthy that Jesus used exactly this idea for His
eschatological proclamation. For it indicates not
simply that we have here eschatological-apocalyptic
prophecy, but more important that man is placed
opposite God, the King and Judge. Thus Jesus
emphasizes very strongly man's complete dependence on God: God can condemn man to hell
(Mt 10[28]) and judges him in accordance with his
behaviour in the face of tasks assigned to him
(Mt 25[14ff]). Yes, God can snatch away the rich
farmer from his possessions before he can enjoy
them (Lk 12[16ff]). Man stands completely insecure
before God, in contrast with whom he can make
no hair black or white, cannot add to his stature,
or lengthen his life (Mt 5[36], 6[27]).

What is the reason for man's unassured dependence on God? It is the fact that man is *created* by
God. Jesus takes this doctrine from the Genesis
account of creation when He is asked to justify

[18] This was first suggested by G. Dalman, *Die Worte Jesu*, I.
(1898).110. Cf. my summary in *Die Eschatologie der Evangelien*
(1936), pp. 6–7.

divorce.[18a] Indeed, Jesus values this conception so highly that He even criticizes the laws of Moses in order to secure the law of creation; man must behave according to the order dictated by God at his creation and because of that no marriage may be dissolved (Mk 10[1ff]).

The fact of the creation of all creatures (Mt 6[30]) is naturally valid, but Jesus does not consider man merely the equal of the animals, but esteems him higher; men are worth more than the birds of the sky and the lilies of the field and many sparrows (Mt 6[26–30], 10[31]). From man's more elevated position within creation, Jesus deduces God's care for man through an *a minori ad maius* conclusion: 'The very hairs of your head are all numbered' (Mt 10[30]). For Jesus, man is certainly the crown of creation, but He does not conclude from that a special value for man in God's eyes but rather man's great obligation. God created man with a special task: man must bring forth fruit (Mt 7[17–19]). Because man is under obligation to do such service to God, Jesus compares him to the slave who comes home tired from the field and then must continue work-

[18a] It seems to me unwarranted to suggest that Jesus in the answer to the question about tribute-money (Mk 12[16–17]) contrasted the image of Caesar on the coin with the image of God given to mankind since creation (= Gen 1[26–7]). This interpretation is made by D. S. Cairns, *The Image of God in Man* (1953), p. 30; also W. Eltester, '*Schöpfungsoffenbarung und natürliche Theologie im frühen Christentum*', *NTSt*, III.(1956–7).97–8; and is regarded as a possible conjecture by J. Jervell, *Imago Dei* (1960), p. 296, note 409.

ing for his master (Lk 17[7ff]). If, like this slave, man were to say after carrying out his duties, 'We are wretched slaves, we have only done what we had to do', this would not mean that man's actions were useless, but rather that man was never anything other than a slave intended for God's service.[19] According to Jesus, man is created for servitude by God because through his actions he is to glorify God; this can be concluded from the fact that the disciples are ordered through their deeds to make others 'see [their] good works and glorify [their] Father which is in heaven' (Mt 5[16]).

Naturally, this picture of man which Jesus gives in His teaching about the Kingdom of God is a picture of man as he *should* be. It is, we must insist, entirely impermissible to attempt to avoid such a picture by excluding as far as possible the representation of God as King and Judge from Jesus' thought.[20] For although Jesus describes God only infrequently as King,[21] yet precisely the choice of the term 'Kingdom of God' for the future time of

---

[19] On the meaning of '*achreios*', as 'poor, needy, wretched' (*armselig*), cf. A. Jülicher (note 9, *supra*), II.21–2; W. Bauer, *Griechisch-deutsches Wörterbuch zu den Schriften des Neuen Testaments und der übrigen urchristlichen Literatur* (5th edn, 1958), p. 255 (ET, *A Greek-English Lexicon of the NT* [1957], p. 128).

[20] So W. Grundmann, *Die Gotteskindschaft in der Geschichte Jesu und ihre religionsgeschichtlichen Voraussetzungen* (1938), pp. 117ff; and J. Leipoldt, *Jesu Verhältnis zu Griechen und Juden* (1941), pp. 131ff.

[21] Doubtless, the King in the parable of the wedding feast (Mt 22[1ff]) is, in the light of Luke 14[16ff], secondary—as W.

salvation shows that Jesus very consciously intends to depict the decisive nature of God by implying Him constantly as 'King'; and one cannot depreciate Jesus' central expectation of the Kingdom (*Basileia*) by recognizing in it only an 'already specified concept'.

Again, the word 'Lord' is seldom used by Jesus of God,[22] but it is significant that in the Parable of the Unfaithful Servant (Mt 18[23ff]), man's position before God is compared to the relationship of a slave to his lord, so that 'master' is clearly a metaphor for God. And in the parable of the slave's work already discussed (Lk 17[7ff]), the position of God as master of men is clearly enough indicated.[23] Also the fact that Jesus sees God as

Michaelis, *Die Gleichnisse Jesu* (1956), pp. 148ff, rightly sees; similarly, J. Jeremias (note 13, *supra*), pp. 56–7 (ET, p. 53). In like manner, the parable of the wicked servant (Mt 18[23ff]) originally featured only a 'Lord' (see Michaelis, op. cit., p. 191). In Matthew 5[35], 'city of the great King' is a quotation from Psalm 47[3], but there is no ground for doubting that Jesus might have consciously taken over this title for God.

[22] See the material in W. Foerster, *ThWb*, III.1085–6; and the critical study by W. Grundmann (note 20, *supra*), pp. 119–20. Apart from quotations from the LXX, whose Semitic equivalent no one can establish in the mouth of Jesus, 'Lord' (*kurios*) is used by Jesus for God in reliably primitive texts only at Matthew 11[25]: 'Father, Lord of heaven and earth', and Matthew 9[38]: 'Lord of the harvest.'

[23] It is entirely arbitrary when W. Grundmann (note 20, *supra*, p. 120) declares: 'This parable also does not make any contribution to the understanding of God!' The central significance of this text for the understanding of Jesus' picture of God has rightly been set out by H. Wegmann, *Feuer auf Erden* (1942), pp. 77–8.

Judge and that He awaited the eschatological judgement follows not only from Jesus' anticipation of
judgement,[24] but also quite clearly from His description of God as the power who can reject
(Mt 10^{28}), and from the parable in Matthew 25^{14ff}
which assumes God as Judge. It is therefore quite
impossible to give a 'modern' interpretation to the
judgement which Jesus anticipated, as if it meant
merely the immanent trial of man against himself.[25]
To Jesus, man is simply God's slave and as a
created being is pledged to the service of God, who
will call him to account.

But man does *not* do God's will. This was clear
in the statements of Jesus mentioned earlier on the
common sinfulness of all men. Now we must add
to them the fact that Jesus took up the typically
Jewish plea for forgiveness in His prayer for the
disciples (Mt 6^{12}). This common sinfulness of all
mankind is even taken into account by Divine Law,
when 'on account of man's hardness of heart' but
in opposition to God's will in creation, the Law
lays down the arrangement of the bill of divorce-
ment (Mk 10^5).

The consequence of this sinfulness of all mankind is not only that man oversteps God's com-
mandment. It also leads to three modes of behaviour in mankind which bring him into explicit
opposition to God.

[24] This is demonstrated in *Promise*, pp. 43ff (Ger. pp. 37ff).
[25] The expositions of W. Grundmann (note 20, *supra*, pp.
121ff) end up in this direction.

(1) Man tries to withdraw from God's command by changing it to suit himself. Because of this, Jesus reproaches the Pharisees: 'How well you set aside what God commands in order to maintain your own tradition' (Mk 7⁹). Because of this, Jesus shows in the antitheses of the Sermon on the Mount (Mt 5²¹ᶠᶠ)—as, indeed, generally in His proclamation of God's command—that the Jews so falsely expounded God's commandments that they became not God's absolute commands but a humanly marked out set of rules, which leave man in fact free at least partially to circumvent God's commandments.

(2) Even worse is a second mode of behaviour in man which Jesus noticed as particularly pronounced among the Pharisees. Man overlooks his slave's position before God and claims special recognition from God by reason of his achievement and cleverness. Jesus depicts this sinful attitude in the parable of the Pharisee and the tax-collector (Lk 18¹⁰ᶠᶠ) and in the previously discussed parable-like admonition to humility before God (Lk 14⁷ᶠᶠ).²⁶ In both texts, tradition has rightly added the interpretatory dictum: 'He who exalts himself will be humbled.' Moreover, the Pharisees are told, with intentional reproof: 'You are the people who get men to think you are good, but God knows what your hearts are! What is lofty in the view of man is loathsome in the eyes of God' (Lk 16¹⁵, Moffatt).

(3) And, finally, the sinful attitude of man is

²⁶ See note 13, *supra.*

shown in that he does not recognize God's care, that he does not want to entrust himself to it; Jesus calls such conduct anxiety, unbelief, fainthearted-ness (Mt 6^{25ff}, Mk 4^{40}, 9^{19}). At its root it simply indicates that man is sinful.

Accordingly, it can hardly be doubted that Jesus sees all men as sinners and that in this, man's sin-fulness, lies the reason why the gospel of the Kingdom of God must be proclaimed.[26a] Man is in inescapable danger of losing his life (Mk 8^{36}) and perishing if he does not repent (Lk 13^{1ff}). All men, indeed, stand in the blind-alley of sin, but it is the fault of the individual if he allows himself to be led astray to sin. 'It is inevitable that hindrances should come, but woe to the man by whom they come' (Lk 17^{1}). It is, therefore, not only Fate but *guilt* whenever man stands before God as sinner.

But now two questions arise which could make our picture of man according to Jesus most dubious.

(I) Does Jesus not have a higher estimation of *the inner man*? We have already seen that the saying regarding the losing of the *psuche* (Mk 8^{36}) may not be utilized to support the idea of the eternal value of the human soul. But elsewhere, too, Jesus does not have a higher regard for the inner man. The admonition, 'Be not anxious about what you are to eat or drink, nor about what you

---

[26a] E. Stauffer, *Die Botschaft Jesu damals und heute* (1951), pp. 45–6, claims that Jesus knew nothing of 'the abominable fairy tale of universal depravity' (*das Greuelmärchen von der allgemeinen Unmoral*). But these texts are not dealt with at all.

are to put on; surely life is more than food and the body more than clothes?' (Mt 6[25]) is only apparently concerned with any antithesis of soul and body. In reality *psuche* is here again a translation for *naphschā* in the sense of 'life'; life and body are both terms for the earthly existence of man, for whose sustenance God, not man, is to care.[27] Similarly, Matthew 10[28], 'Fear not those who kill the body but cannot kill the *psuche*; rather fear Him who can destroy both *psuche* and body in Gehenna', is not intended to designate the value of the immortal soul, but rather to emphasize that only God can destroy the heavenly life as distinct from the earthly.[28]

One could sooner find a higher value for the inner man in the Gethsemane scene, 'the spirit is willing but the flesh is weak' (Mk 14[38]). But the determination of the age of this saying is most uncertain. Today, this admonition to all disciples, or indeed to all peoples, is often considered to be an intrusion of the later Church's theology into the Gethsemane scene.[29] But this assumption is very

[27] See the exposition of A. Schlatter, *Der Evangelist Matthäus* (2nd edn, 1933), pp. 227–8, and J. Schniewind, *Das Evangelium nach Matthäus* (1937), p. 90.

[28] See the Commentaries by Schlatter and Schniewind (note 27, *supra*), *ad loc*. The absence of *psuche* in the parallel Luke 12[4] is doubtless a secondary variation (so rightly F. Hauck, *Das Evangelium des Lukas* [1934], p. 165).

[29] So Bultmann (note 10, *supra*), p. 288; J. Finegan, *Die Ueberlieferung der Leidens- und Auferstehungsgeschichte Jesu* (1934), p. 70; H. Lietzmann, *ZNW*, XXX.(1931).212; J. Sundwall (note 11, *supra*), p. 81; F. Hauck, *Das Evangelium des Markus*

improbable, because as Lohmeyer has rightly observed,[30] Jesus' rebuke to the sleeping disciples (Mk 14[37]) finds its basis in the reference in 14[38] to the eschatological temptation which is now being fulfilled. Even if 14[38] does belong to the original Gethsemane report, since we have no reliable witnesses for the proceedings we cannot be certain that in Mark 14[32ff] we have a report which is trustworthy in all its details, even if we cannot easily question the historicity of the whole scene.[31] But even were the rendering of Mark 14[38] more certain than it is, this sentence would not show that Jesus regarded the inner man as standing closer to God than the outer man. For if a contradiction in man is acknowledged here, it is only in the sense that man does not always strive undividedly against

---

(1931), p. 172; E. Klostermann, *Das Markus-Evangelium* (3rd edn, 1936), p. 149; R. Meyer, *Der Prophet aus Galiläa* (1940), p. 141; H. Braun, *Spätjüdisch-häretischer und frühchristlicher Radikalismus* II.(1957).116, note 4.

[30] E. Lohmeyer, *Das Markus-Evangelium* (1937), p. 317. The exclusion of verse 38 is similarly opposed by H. J. Ebeling, *Das Messiasgeheimnis und die Botschaft des Marcus-Evangelisten* (1939), p. 176; K. G. Kuhn, 'Jesus in Gethsemane', *ETh*, XII.(1952/3). 275.

[31] So rightly J. Schniewind (note 16, *supra*), p. 178; F. Hauck (note 29, *supra*), p. 172; J. Finegan (note 29, *supra*), pp. 70–1; H. Lietzmann, *ZNW*, XXX.(1931).212; E. Schweizer, '*Die sieben Geister in der Apokalypse*', *ETh*, (1951/2).507; V. Taylor, *Mark*, p. 551; E. Schweizer, *ThWb*, VI.394, VII.123–4. The legendary character of the whole story is urged by R. Bultmann, *Geschichte*, p. 288; M. Dibelius (note 10, *supra*, pp. 212ff), who sees the root of the whole account in the traditional word of Jesus in 14[38]; also R. Meyer (note 29, *supra*), p. 141.

God, in spite of the fact, however, that he is answerable as a whole man before God.[32] The evil is not in the lesser self which drags down the higher self, but in the human will which sets itself against God's will in spite of the possible opposition of the 'spirit'. 'Man's sensuality is not the evil thing in him. The whole man is evil when his will is evil.'[33]

Thus our interpretation of Jesus' view of the common sinfulness of man cannot be weakened by the suggestion of any anthropological dualism in Jesus.

(2) A second question is even more essential for our consideration. Does not Jesus' view of man as the *child of God* imply that he is especially valuable to God? There has been a recent tendency, as already mentioned, to see the nature of God in the preaching of Jesus as identified only with the image of the Father. If this were correct, would it not follow that for Jesus all men are the children of God? J. Leipoldt therefore asks whether Matthew 5[45], 'that you might become sons of your Father who is in heaven', could not be translated as 'that you may show yourselves as children of God', yet thinks this interpretation to be uncertain and de-

---

[32] Mark 14[38] does not indicate the opposition between human nature and divine spirit, as Schniewind (note 16, *supra*, p. 178) and V. Taylor (*Mark*, p. 555) think; but rather the Old Testament opposition between human will and human action. So E. Lohmeyer (note 30, *supra*), p. 317; E. de Witt Burton (note 3, *supra*), p. 179; and K. G. Kuhn (note 30, *supra*), p. 276.

[33] R. Bultmann, *Jesus* (1926), pp. 46-7.

clares that it is unfortunately doubtful whether in Jesus' opinion 'all men are by nature children of God'.[34] Now there can be no question that Jesus proclaimed God as the Father of mankind with especial emphasis.[35] However, W. Michaelis has shown[36] that beside the many sayings of Jesus concerning God the Father there are to be found only very few which refer to man as the child of God. Such are: 'Blessed are the peacemakers: for they shall be called the children of God' (Mt 5[9]), and 'Love your enemies . . . that you may become sons of your Father in heaven' (Mt 5[44-5]). Luke 20[36], which states that the resurrected 'cannot die any more for they are equal unto the angels; and are the children of God, being the children of the resurrection', is questionable as a saying of Jesus, being undoubtedly an extension of Mark 12[25]: 'but they are as the angels which are in heaven.'

However, these few utterances clearly show man's sonship of God only as an *eschatological gift*. So Luke 6[35] in the parallel to Matthew 5[45] has rightly 'and you shall be sons of the Highest'. In no way does Jesus therefore assume that men are by nature

[34] J. Leipoldt (note 20, *supra*), pp. 140–1.
[35] Cf. my article in *Judaica*, I.(1945).53ff.
[36] '*Das Urchristentum*', in *Mensch und Gottheit in den Religionen* (1942), pp. 322–3. Ernst Percy (*Die Botschaft Jesu* [Lunds Universitets Årsskrift N.F. Avd. 1, Bd. 49, Nr. 5] [1953], p. 114, note 3) attacks incorrectly the eschatological character of man's sonship to God, on the grounds of the Fatherhood of God. P. I. Bratsiotis (note 5, *supra*, p. 26) does the same, with reference to its psychological impossibility.

the children of God. Rather, according to Jesus, man awaits the transition into becoming a child of God *through God's deed*, if he allows himself to be called to repentance by his meeting with Jesus and then turns to do the will of God. Being a child of God is not the presupposition but the eschatological fulfilment of the saving act of God.

If one combines all the previously discussed characteristics of Jesus' picture of man, it is quite clear that Jesus developed no one *theory* of man, but that a very definite picture of man stood behind His gospel preaching. Jesus does not see man either as naturally related to God, or in the dichotomy between nature and spirit. He sees man as an active person, standing over against God but failing to fulfil his task which is the service of God. Therefore Jesus sees man as a historical being,[37] caught between his creation in the past and his judgement in the future. Thus it is only logical that Jesus describes salvation as a historical act of God which places man before a new possibility within his historical existence, and makes free for him the way to salvation. It could easily be shown that Jesus' whole preaching of salvation implies and

[37] I use the concept of 'historicity' in this connexion in a sense similar to W. Bachmann (note 1, *supra*, pp. 43–4); although Bachmann himself does not co-ordinate this concept into the New Testament concept of salvation-history culminating in Jesus. For this, see O. Cullmann, *Christus und die Zeit* (1946; ET, *Christ and Time* [1950]), *passim*; further, W. G. Kümmel, *'Futurische und präsentische Eschatologie im ältesten Urchristentum'*, *NTSt*, V.(1959).113ff.

confirms this picture of man, based as it is on the new situation within the whole salvation history which the works of Jesus have inaugurated.[38] But such a larger demonstration is not possible here.

[38] On this, see my arguments in *Promise*, pp. 141ff (Ger. pp. 133ff).

THREE

Paul

THE QUESTION now arises how the Pauline view stands in relation to that of Jesus. Paul is, indeed, particularly important, for he is the only New Testament writer who to any great extent offers us direct statements about man's nature, and uses extensively the anthropological terminology of his time. Paul's anthropological statements have, therefore, always determined quite decisively the whole picture of man which Christian doctrine has extracted from the New Testament.[39] It is to be questioned, furthermore, whether the Pauline picture of man differs essentially from Jesus' conception.

It is extremely difficult to describe Paul's anthropology, both because he uses a series of anthropological terms in his description of human existence which are not clearly defined one from the other, and also because he uses these terms in a quite careless way.[40] Ever since H. Lüdemann's

[39] For example, the mainly constructive essay of H. Schlier (note 5, *supra*) is built exclusively on the words of Paul. Similarly, H. D. Wendland (note 5, *supra*) confines himself almost entirely to Paul.

[40] This has been pointed out also by K. Th. Schaefer (note 5, *supra*, pp. 25–6), and H. Mehl-Koehnlein (note 6, *supra*, p. 5). S. Leuchli (note 6, *supra*) goes even farther, and states that, even

basic work,[41] the attempt has been made to read a metaphysical dualism in the Pauline view of man.[42] The 'history of religions school' has thus further explained Paul's anthropology as founded upon ecstatic experience, and therefore most closely related to hellenistic mysticism.[43] Both explanations are false, as has been already emphasized many times,[44] and the careful exposition of Pauline anthropology by W. Gutbrod (1934) avoids these extremes.[44a] Gutbrod may be referred to for all terminological details. Here, we shall only attempt to place Paul's anthropological views within the collective framework of his whole preaching of salvation.

in more recent studies, 'the Pauline anthropology is not fully solved, because it is not fully solved in Paul. And perhaps it is not solved in Paul simply because Paul did not intend to solve it. He was not interested in anthropology.' And if, as doubtless happened, Paul 'could take over some Hellenistic views of man into his Rabbinic background' (p. 27), that does not mean that he *must* have taken over the original meaning of the terminology.

[41] *Die Anthropologie des Paulus und ihre Stellung innerhalb seiner Heilslehre* (1872).

[42] Cf. writers like C. Holsten (*Das Evangelium des Paulus*, II. [1899].38–9), H. J. Holtzmann (note 9, *supra*, II.21, 42ff), and those named by W. Schauf (note 6, *supra*, p. 18, note 4).

[43] So W. Bousset (*Kyrios Christos* [2nd edn, 1921], pp. 126ff), R. Reitzenstein (*Die hellenistischen Mysterienreligionen* [3rd edn, 1927], pp. 333ff).

[44] R. Bultmann, *G.u.V.*, I.(1933).129; W. G. Kümmel, *Bekehrung*, 21ff; W. Schauf (note 6, *supra*, pp. 172ff); W. D. Davies, *Paul and Rabbinic Judaism* (1948), pp. 17ff; H. Mehl-Koehnlein (note 6, *supra*, p. 15); J. A. T. Robinson (note 6, *supra*, p. 24); O. Kuss (note 6, *supra*, pp. 527ff); E. Schweizer, *ThWb*, VII.135–6.

[44a] The same applies to W. D. Stacey (note 6, *supra*).

Paul sees man as a member of the *kosmos* (Rom 1⁸, 3¹⁹, 11¹²,¹⁵, 1 Cor 1²⁰⁻¹,²⁷⁻⁸, 4¹³, 6², 2 Cor 1¹², 5¹⁷, Col 1⁶) and therewith as a created being (1 Cor 11⁹; cf. Rom 9²⁰ᶠᶠ, Col 1²³). As a creature of God, man must recognize himself as standing over against God, and give honour to God as God (*hōs Theon doxazein*) (Rom 1²¹). His attitude, however, is the opposite of this; man refuses to acknowledge God and allows himself to be determined by the powers of the *kosmos* and by human traditions (Rom 1²¹, 1 Cor 1²¹, 2¹², Col 2⁸). Like Jesus, Paul sees man exclusively as a being standing over against God,⁴⁵ a being whose real vocation of service to God is opposed to his actual slavery to the creation (*ktisis*) (Rom 1²⁵), a slavery which shows itself in 'boasting' (*kauchasthai*) (1 Cor 1²⁷ᶠᶠ).⁴⁶

⁴⁵ The same conclusion would arise out of a consideration of Paul's use of the concept *anthropos*, which almost always describes man as over against God (e.g. Rom 1¹⁸, 3⁴, 14¹⁸, 1 Cor 1²⁵, 2 Cor 5¹¹, 1 Thess 2⁴, 4⁸, etc.). Only in a few cases (Rom 1²³, 1 Cor 4⁹, 13¹, 15³⁹) does man appear as 'of worldly nature' beside other creatures, and perhaps this is due to the fact that only man's having been created is in these texts in question, and not his belonging to the *kosmos* which is far from God. Similarly, that Paul considers man always as standing before God is confirmed by his use of '*kata anthropon*' (Rom 3⁵, 1 Cor 3⁹, 9⁸, Gal 1¹¹, 3¹⁵) and '*anthropinos*' (Rom 6¹⁹, 1 Cor 2¹³, 4³, 10¹³). Cf. on these concepts R. Bultmann, *RGG*, IV.(2nd edn, 1930). 1031–2; R. Bultmann, *Theology*, pp. 230–1, 254ff (Ger. pp. 231–2, 254ff); W. Gutbrod (note 6, *supra*), pp. 19ff.

⁴⁶ Cf. further, Romans 4²: (Abraham) has cause for pride (*kauchema*), but not before God; 1 Corinthians 3²¹: Never make men a ground for pride; 2 Corinthians 11¹⁷: I do not speak 'as a Christian' (*NEB*) in this confidence of boasting. R. Bultmann, *ThWb*, III.648ff, shows that 'to boast according to the flesh'

Paul sees man trapped by the *kosmos*, standing distinct from God, set in the midst of the great antithesis of *sarx* and *pneuma*.

What does Paul mean by *sarx*? First, he can use the word quite unemphatically, as an indication of the natural man and his corporeality, and thus simply denoting his earthly origin (1 Cor 1[29], Rom 3[20], Gal 1[16], Rom 1[3]).[47] But '*sarx*' is more frequently used to indicate the opposite of God or '*pneuma*', and it then denotes the *whole* man, who faces the Creator as a sinner. So Romans 7[14], 8[4], 1 Corinthians 3[3]: Are you not still fleshly (*sarkikoi*), and walking according to man? Man as *sarx* is therefore a sinner. So Romans 7[14]: I am fleshly, 'the purchased slave of sin' (*NEB*).

This connexion of *sarx* with sin has often been understood as if Paul regarded man as sinful simply because of his attachment to material things.[47a] That is undoubtedly wrong. Paul does not think that sin is naturally bound up with *sarx*. One can live 'in the flesh' (*en sarki*), without fighting 'according to the flesh' (*kata sarka*) (2 Cor 10[3]). The sinfulness of the *sarx* does not belong to it

(2 Cor 11[18]) is synonymous with 'to put confidence in (*pepoithe-nai*) the flesh' (Phil 3[4]), so that self-glorying manifests itself in grounding oneself in one's fleshly nature.

[47] Cf. on this and on what follows above the summaries in Kümmel, *Bekehrung*, pp. 16ff; O. Kuss (note 6, *supra*), pp. 506ff; Bultmann, *Theology*, I. 232ff (Ger. pp. 232ff); E. Schweizer, *ThWb*, VII.124ff.

[47a] So again J. Klausner, *From Jesus to Paul* (1943), p. 522; H. Preisker, *Das Ethos des Urchristentums* (1949), p. 179.

42   MAN IN THE NEW TESTAMENT

simply because it is bodily, earthly existence.[48]
That Paul does not refer the connexion between
sarx and sin back to *sarx* as material body is shown
especially in the fact that he does not see any
dualism inside man which contrasts *sarx* as the
lower part of man with a higher inner man related
to God. It has often been pointed out that Paul
knew the Greek dualism of outer and inner man.
Indeed, the whole Pauline anthropology has been
seen as founded on this antithesis.[49] However, by

[48] The terminology of Paul is obviously not consistent: Paul
can denote also the sinful life by '*en sarki*' (Rom 7[5], 8[8–9]), and
can use '*kata sarka*' simply to indicate physical origin (Rom 1[3],
4[1], 1 Cor 10[18], etc.). W. D. Davies (note 44, *supra*, p. 18)
thinks that '*sarx*' would not be used like '*hule*' as a means of
denoting 'the material'. However, the 'post-Epicurean word-
history' associates flesh = material body with sin, opposed to
spirit; although Paul shows no influence from this development
(see E. Schweizer, *ZNW*, XLVIII.[1957].250–1, and *ThWb*,
VII.104, 132–3). Moreover, Davies (p. 163) makes it quite clear
that *sarx* in the deprecatory sense occurs in Paul relatively
seldom, and then only in certain connexions (most important,
Rom 7 and 8, Col 2[11–12], Gal 5[13ff]). D. Flusser, 'The Dead Sea
Sect and Pre-Pauline Christianity', *Scripta Hierosolymitana*, IV.
(1958).254ff, shows that the opposition between unredeemed
man as flesh and the Spirit of God in Qumran as in the New
Testament 'differs basically from the Greek and Gnostic view
which regards both spirit and matter as elements inherent in the
world in general and man in particular'.

[49] See those referred to in Kümmel, *Bekehrung*, p. 14, note 1,
and A. Schlatter, *Die Theologie der Apostel* (2nd edn, 1922),
p. 267: 'Because of the disastrous influence which the flesh
exerts upon us, our "inner man" is the better part of us, which
Divine grace seeks to renew'; also S. Laeuchli (note 6, *supra*),
pp. 19–20. Correct on this point are Ernst Käsemann, *Leib und
Leib Christi* (1933), p. 122, Gutbrod, pp. 85ff, Althaus, p. 41,

'the inner man', Paul means (2 Cor 4[16]) the *renewed
being of the Christian*. Romans 7[22] deals with the
natural man who agrees to God's will according to
his inner man, but there is no thought here, as we
shall show, of any antithesis between the inner man
which is peculiarly near to God on the one hand,
and the earthly body on the other. Only an examination of the terms Paul uses for the spiritual man
could show whether Paul thinks of a dualism of
this kind in the inner man.[50]

Unfortunately, accurate and relative definitions
of the different terms for the inner man as used by
Paul (*psuche, nous, noema, kardia, pneuma, suneidesis, dianoia, splagchna, phrenes*) are *a priori* impossible, for the terms do not denote psychologically
different functions, but are used promiscuously.[50a]
Psuche, 'soul', is already clearly placed on the side
of *sarx*, as Paul denotes the earthly man separate
from God, unable to understand the divine
pneuma, with *psuchikos* as well as with *sarkikos*
(1 Cor 2[13–14], 15[44–5]). The *nous*, 'mind', of man,
again, is called 'fleshly' (*nous tes sarkos*) and
'reprobate' (*adokimos nous*) (Col 2[18], Rom 1[28]), and
Paul demands its regeneration. However, Paul

note 4, and Stacey, pp. 211–12 (see note 6, *supra*, for Titles);
Bultmann, *Theology*, I.203–4, 206–7 (Ger. pp. 204, 207).

[50] For references, see Kümmel, *Bekehrung*, pp. 26ff.

[50a] S. Laeuchli (note 6, *supra*, p. 17) suggests that in 1 Corinthians 14[14–15] Paul makes 'a very definite differentiation: *pneuma*
and *nous* are here precisely not identical'. But this overlooks the
fact that *pneuma* denotes the Divine Spirit, and is not an
anthropological concept.

speaks of the fact that man can with his *nous* perceive the eternal power of God and His divinity (Rom 1[20]), and insists that man with his *nous* confirms the law of God, even while his members are at the service of sin (Rom 7[23, 25b]). It will immediately be asked if Paul does not assume thereby a higher side in man which is related to God.

It is even more difficult to answer the question of *pneuma*, 'spirit', as an indication of the inner man. That Paul can use *pneuma* as an anthropological term is shown when he expresses his distress at Titus' absence once with *pneuma* ('I still found no relief for my spirit', 2 Cor 2[13]) and once with *sarx* ('our flesh had no relief', 2 Cor 7[5]). Moreover, Paul also speaks of a 'spirit (*pneuma*) of the man which is in him' (1 Cor 2[11]). But these places in which *pneuma* denotes the inner man are few and unterminological and the context shows that this human *pneuma* stands in no way particularly close to God, but rather belongs entirely to the side of *sarx*.

Does 1 Thessalonians 5[23] go against this? There we find written in a formal benediction, 'and the God of peace sanctify you wholly; and I pray God your whole spirit and soul and body be preserved blameless unto the coming of our Lord Jesus Christ'. There appears to be a trichotomy here, with a distinction between *psuche* as the lower and *pneuma* as the higher function of man's inner life. But that would be very strange, and one must either accept that Paul, without further thought, places *psuche* and *pneuma* beside one another here in a liturgical form, without the *pneuma* being distinguished in any way as standing closer to God,[51] or else one must (which is more probable) relate *pneuma* here to the Divine Spirit accorded to Christians.[52]

From the remaining terms which Paul uses as distinguishing marks of the inner man,[53] one could

[51] So also Gutbrod (note 6, *supra*), pp. 90-1; M. Dibelius, *An die Thessalonicher*, I.II, *An die Philipper* (3rd edn, 1937), p. 32; Stacey (note 6, *supra*), p. 123; B. Rigaux, *Les Épîtres aux Thessaloniciens* (1956), p. 599; Bultmann, *Theology*, p. 207 (Ger. pp. 206-7); E. Schweizer, *ThZ*, IX.(1953).76, and *ThWb*, VI.433; also C. Guignebert (note 4, *supra*), pp. 430-1. It has been suggested that the distinction between *psuche* and *pneuma* should be understood as that between the animal and the spiritual 'life principle' (*Lebensprinzip*)—so K. Th. Schaefer (note 5, *supra*), p. 27; similarly, K. L. Schmidt, *Ein Gang durch den Galaterbrief* (1942), pp. 64-5; M. Goguel, *La naissance du Christianisme* (1946), p. 255; P. I. Bratsiosis (note 5, *supra*), p. 29. This, however, is very difficult to demonstrate. In any case, this distinction cannot establish that the spirit as a 'spiritual principle' stands closer to God. Even more is the suggestion impossible, that *pneuma* here could denote the whole man, and *psuche* and *soma* its parts (so C. Masson, *Les deux Épîtres de Saint Paul aux Thessaloniciens* (1957), pp. 77-8).

[52] So E. von Dobschütz, *Die Thessalonicherbriefe* (1909), p. 229; Ernst Fuchs, *Christus und der Geist bei Paulus* (1932), pp. 42-3.

[53] *Noema* means, when not used of the Christian, the godless mind of man (2 Cor 3^{14}, 4^4) or of Satan (2 Cor 2^{11}). Cf. J. Behm, *ThWb*, IV.959. *Dianoia* is used in Colossians 1^{21} for the mind of the Colossian Christians as it was when formerly alien to God. *Splagchna* is used only for the inner life of Christians (2 Cor 6^{12}, 7^{15}, Phil 1^8, 2^1, Col 3^{12}, Philem 7, 12, 20), although without any suggestion of a contrast with the outer man. *Phrenes* occurs only in 1 Corinthians 14^{20}, in the sense of 'understanding', to denote an answerable rather than a merely sinful or culpable action.

at the most bring forward *kardia* as a proof for the inner man's especial nearness to God. It is said of the heathen that they have the law written in their hearts, when they fulfil the demands of the law (Rom 2[15]), and the *kardia* appears as the place in man where belief originates (Rom 10[10]). Now *kardia* is doubtless for Paul the organ 'where the meeting between God and man takes place, and indeed in both respects—whether man shuts himself off from God or opens himself to Him'.[54] But even if *kardia* denotes the inner man in his most personal being, this heart does not in any way stand in antithesis to an outer man who is farther from God, but describes precisely the *whole* man to his very depths (2 Cor 5[12]: *prosopon* indicates man centred on himself and *kardia* man centred on God). And, besides, it is precisely the *kardia* of the natural man which is 'senseless', the seat of ungodly passions, disinclined to repentance, far from the knowledge of divine revelation (Rom 1[21, 24], 2[5], 1 Cor 2[9], 2 Cor 3[15]).

Suneidesis is used most frequently—fifteen times, as much in the sense of the moral self-consciousness (Rom 13[5]) as in that of moral decision (1 Cor 10[25ff]). This ability to make moral decisions is common to all men (Rom 2[15]), but cannot stand secure in the face of God's judgement (2 Cor 4[2], 5[11]). Cf. Gutbrod (note 6, *supra*), pp. 55ff; C. A. Pierce, *Conscience in the New Testament* (1955); Bultmann, *Theology I*, pp. 216ff (Ger. pp. 217ff). None of these infrequently used concepts suggests that the inner man has any special value in the eyes of God.

[54] Gutbrod (note 6, *supra*), p. 71; Bultmann, *Theology I*, pp. 220–1 (Ger. pp. 221–2).

From the examination of these terms used to denote the inner man, it is clear that Paul knows no human inner life related to God but only the complete man, who *is sarx, soma, psuche,* etc., and wholly stands over against God.

However, as already mentioned, Paul seems also to make statements which assume the inner man's especial nearness to God. He speaks of the fact that man with the *nous* can recognize the Creator from creation (Rom 1[20]), that the heathen have God's law written in their hearts and that the heathen's conscience confirms this fact (Rom 2[15]). Again, Paul speaks of the agreement of the *nous* with the divine law, whilst the members combat this law (Rom 7[14ff]). We must now consider these three texts in more detail.

(1) *Romans 1[19-20]*. It might be unquestionably assumed that the implication here is that man can, by his *nous*, discern from the created world the invisible God, who since the beginning of creation revealed therein His power and divinity. However, this must be seen in the light of the whole passage Rom 1[19] to 3[20], in which it is made quite clear that the whole of mankind is quite lost apart from the revelation of God's righteousness in Christ. Consequently, the thought expressed in 1[19-20] can only serve to show the inexcusability of man who has *known* God but has not wanted to *acknowledge* Him. Paul concedes that the *nous* could lead man to God, and because of that man would be under an obligation to know something of God and to bow down

before God: but in reality man does not allow himself to be led to God through his knowledge of God from creation. The possibility that he might remains unfulfilled.[55]

(2) *Romans* 2^{14-15}. Here, it is said of the heathen that each time they fulfil the demands of the law, they show that some ordinances of the divine law are already inscribed in their hearts; and that the conscience of the heathen which passes judgement on the rightness of an action only confirms this inner knowledge of the demands of the law. Here, too, Paul concedes the possibility that the heathen sometimes carry out God's will, because they know about it by nature. But here, too, this thought—in the formulation of which Paul follows Hellenistic trains of thought[56]—does not serve to show the nearness to God of the inner man but merely places the heathen as unpardonable before God's judgement if they have not really done God's will. Thus, 'revelation through creation' or 'natural

[55] Althaus (note 6, *supra*, p. 44, note 3, p. 46) has rightly objected to my earlier remarks (*Bekehrung*, p. 28) that Paul does not here speak 'purely hypothetically', but on the contrary delineates actual man, who stands in opposition to his God-given commission. The striking character of this thought, so far as Paul's anthropology is concerned, is in part to be explained by Paul's dependence upon Hellenistic conceptions. Cf. G. Bornkamm, '*Die Offenbarung des Zornes Gottes (Rom 1–3)*', *ZNW*, XXXIV.(1935).239ff, esp. pp. 243–4 = *Das Ende des Gesetzes* (1952), pp. 9ff, esp. pp. 13–14.

[56] See the examples from Stoicism in J. von Arnim, *Stoicorum veterum fragmenta*, Vol. III, Nos. 308ff.

revelation'[57] in Paul does not demonstrate the *nearness* to God *of the inner man*, but rather the great *distance* from Him in which the *whole* man stands. For man, who as a created being knows God's demands in his innermost heart, yet has not carried out these demands.

(3) *Romans 7[14ff]*. Most striking of all is this description of the antithesis in man, inwardly affirming God's will but outwardly transgressing from it:

For we know that the law is spiritual: but I am carnal sold under sin.

For that which I do I know not: for not what I would, that do I practise; but what I hate that I do.

But if what I would not that I do, I consent unto the Law that it is good.

[57] (Ger. *Schöpfungsoffenbarung*). So Brunner (note 1, *supra*), p. 543; also *Offenbarung und Vernunft* (1941), pp. 59ff. Brunner rightly points out that no *theologia naturalis* is to be understood on the basis of Paul's teaching of 'revelation through creation'. Paul clearly excludes the possibility that men, to whom such 'revelation through creation' holds out the knowledge of God, would actually desire to know Him—and precisely here is man's inexcusability grounded. And when Cullmann (note 37, *supra*, pp. 159ff) says that the revelation through the work of creation 'from the point of view of Christ is already Christian revelation', so also, in view of the statement from faith that everything was created through Christ (Col 1[16]), is that doubtless correct for Paul. But that is, of course, only demonstrable retrospectively, on the basis of faith in Christ. The inexcusability of mankind outside of Christ is itself based rather on the fact that the revelation through creation 'is none other than that which at the beginning of all things went out to all mankind as a summons to

The answer to the question of whether nevertheless a contradiction in man is maintained, assuming a greater nearness to God in the inner man, depends on what is the actual subject of Romans 7[14ff].

Romans 7[14ff] depicts in the present tense and in the first person the desperate state of a man who in spite of a desire to the contrary must bow to the dictates of the law of sin in his members, and does not get farther than the hopeless cry: 'O wretched man that I am. Who will deliver me from the body of this death?' (7[24]). As this description in the present tense follows a section which similarly describes in the first person the *origin* of this condition, depicted as past happening (7[7–13]), it might seem quite natural to see in 7[14ff] a description of the present experience of Paul the Christian, and hence of all Christians. If this opinion, defended by Ambrose and Augustine and especially by the Reformers and found even to the present day, were right, then Romans 7[14ff] would not need to be referred to for the understanding of Paul's picture of *man* as such, and the difficulty that this text seems to posit a special nearness to God of the

the recognition of human impotency (Rom 1[21])—and thus belongs to the Christ line' (Cullmann, p. 160). In actual *content*, however, this was not revelation. We may summarize the matter in Pauline language by saying that the revelation through creation *should* have left man able to know God, but that men stifled this knowledge (*katechein*, Rom 1[18]; 'the world failed to find Him by its wisdom', 1 Cor 1[21] *NEB*), and thus were guilty, so that God now by way of the foolishness of the Cross and through faith in Christ justifies man (1 Cor 1[21], Rom 3[21–2]).

inner man would not need any special explanation.
However, ever since Tertullian and Origen, this
interpretation has often been rejected as impossible,
and Romans 7[14ff] has been referred to the *non*-
Christian whose condition is portrayed in the style
of the first person and seen with the eyes of the
Christian. This view which I earlier propounded[58]
has found no little agreement.[59] But precisely be-

---

[58] *Bekehrung*, esp. pp. 118ff.

[59] Cf. G. Kuhlmann, *Theologia naturalis bei Philon und bei
Paulus* (1930), p. 95; Th. Schlatter, *Für Gott lebendig in Christi
Kraft, Jahrbuch der Theologischen Schule Bethel* (1930), pp.
137–8; R. Bultmann, *ThR*, VI.(1934).233, also '*Römer 7
und die Anthropologie des Paulus*', *Imago Dei, Festschrift für
G. Krüger* (1932), pp. 53ff; Gutbrod (note 6, *supra*), pp. 52–3,
166; A. Schlatter, *Gottes Gerechtigkeit* (1935), pp. 249–50; E.
Brunner, *Der Römerbrief* (1938), pp. 54–5; W. Grundmann,
ThWb, I.315, note 157; G. Schrenk, *ThWb*, III.50; P. Althaus
(note 6, *supra*), pp. 31ff, also '*Zur Auslegung von Röm. 7.14ff*',
ThLZ (1952), pp. 475ff; E. Delay, '*Une question d'anthropologie
à propos de Rom. VII*', *Revue de théologie et de philosophie*,
XXVIII.(1940).335ff; Schlier (note 5, *supra*), p. 28; E. Gaugler,
Der Römerbrief, I.(1945).213ff; E. Fuchs, *Die Freiheit des
Glaubens* (1949), pp. 80–1; A. Feuillet, '*Le plan salvifique de
Dieu d'après l'Épître aux Romains*', *Revue Biblique*, LVII.(1950).
368ff; Mehl-Koehnlein (note 6, *supra*), p. 25; G. Bornkamm,
'*Sünde, Gesetz und Tod (Röm. 7)*', in *Das Ende des Gesetzes* (1952),
pp. 51ff; E. Haenchen, '*Das Buch Baruch*', *ZThK*, L.(1953).
151; A. Brunot, *Le génie littéraire de Saint Paul* (1955), p. 153;
F.-J. Leenhardt, *L'Épître de Saint Paul aux Romains* (1957),
pp. 104–5, 112–13; K. G. Kuhn (note 4, *supra*), pp. 102–3;
W. Matthias (note 6, *supra*), p. 389; J. Huby, *Saint Paul, Épître
aux Romains* (Nouvelle édition par S. Lyonnet, 1957), pp. 255–6;
C. K. Barrett, *A Commentary on the Epistle to the Romans* (1957),
p. 152; H. Braun, '*Römer 7.7–25 und das Selbstverständnis des
Qumran-Frommen*', *ZThK*, LVI.(1959).1ff; Kuss (note 6,
supra), pp. 478, 482–3; Nelson (note 6, *supra*), p. 19; E.

cause of the relationship of Romans 7[14ff] to other
anthropological views of Paul, it has also been
sharply contested. Consequently, the thesis has
been revived that Romans 7[14ff] portrays the Christian man, since only on this assumption can the
contradiction of this text to Paul's view of the
natural man be explained.[60] Alternatively, which

Schweizer, *ThWb*, VII.133-4; probably also S. B. Yun, *Römer
7.25 und der Pneumatikos* (1958).

E. Stauffer (*ThWb*, II.355ff, and *Die Theologie des Neuen
Testaments* [4th edn, 1948], p. 253, note 239 [ET. tr. *New
Testament Theology* (1955), p. 275, note 239]) wishes to interpret
Romans 7 in a 'salvation history' sense, meaning the Jewish
people under the Law (similarly A. Kirchgässner, *Erlösung und
Sünde im Neuen Testament* [1950], pp. 34-5). This amounts to the
same, so far as the anthropological ideas of Romans 7[14ff] are
concerned, but is in itself an unclear and exegetically improbable
interpretation. (With R. Bultmann, *ThR*, VI.(1934).233, note 1.)
I find quite unintelligible the view of E. Percy (*Die Probleme der
Kolosser-und Epheserbriefe* [*Skrifter utg. av Kungl. Humanistiska
Vetenskapssamfundet i Lund*, XXXIX] [1946], pp. 304-5), who
identifies 'the situation of the man standing under the Law, as
Paul from his own experience as a Christian sees it', with the
'Christian, as he is in himself, apart from his new existence in
Christ'. Romans 7[7ff] is still understood purely psychologically
by O. Pfister (*Das Christentum und die Angst* [1944], pp. 187-8);
C. H. Dodd (*St Paul's Epistle to the Romans* [1932 (= 12th edn,
1949)], pp. 108ff); J. W. Bowman (*The Religion of Maturity*
[1948], pp. 263-4); Klausner ([note 47a, *supra*], pp. 498-9);
Davies ([note 44, *supra*], pp. 23ff), and Stacey ([note 6, *supra*],
p. 212).

[60] O. Moe (note 4, *supra*), pp. 389-90; H. Möller, '*Römer 7
ist und bleibt das Bild des Christen*', Dtsch. Theol. (1939), pp. 5ff,
68ff; Chr. Maurer, *Die Gesetzeslehre des Paulus* (1941), pp. 43ff,
52-3, 104; A. Nygren, *Der Römerbrief* (1951), pp. 208ff; M.
Magnusson, *Der Begriff 'Verstehen' in exegetischem Zusammen-
hang unter besonderer Berücksichtigung der paulinischen Schriften*

from the anthropological point of view comes to
the same thing, Romans 7^{14ff} has been described as
the experience of the Christian Church.[61]

We cannot here repeat the considerations from
the relationship of the text to its context and from
its comparison with the remaining Pauline writings
in favour of the hypothesis that the form of the
first person in Romans 7$^{7-25}$ is a stylistic form for
the portrayal of *human experience* in general and
that this portrayal must be referred to the non-
Christians. Here, our problem is whether the interpretation of the text as portraying non-Christians
does in fact remove Romans 7^{14ff} from the general
frame of Pauline anthropology. Particularly, what
place has the text within the common framework
if it in fact must be understood as a description of

(1954), pp. 151ff; W. Nauck, *Die Tradition und der Charakter
des 1. Johannesbriefes* (1957), p. 107. C. L. Mitton ('Romans VII
Reconsidered', *ExpT*, LXV.[1953/4].78ff, 99ff, 132ff) finds the
Christian who falls back into reliance upon the Law described.
However, the text says nothing about such 'reliance upon the
Law'! L. Goppelt (*Christentum und Judentum im ersten und
zweiten Jahrhundert* [1954], p. 106) relates the text to the *past*
of the Christian, which lies always beneath him, rather than
simply behind him in a temporal sense. According to E. Ellwein
('*Das Rätsel von Römer VII*', *Kerygma und Dogma*, I.[1955].
247ff) Romans 7 speaks of a 'progress' in the Christian life from
the received gift of freedom from sin and the Law to the
constantly renewed further presentation of that gift to him. No
exegetical proof is offered for this view!
[61] A. F. W. Lekkerkerker, '*Romeinen 7, een belijdenis der
gemeente*', *Nieuwe Theol. Studiën*, XXIII.(1940), pp. 99ff; and
Römer 7 und Römer 9 bei Augustin (Diss. Utrecht, 1942), pp. 68ff.
(Latter volume cited below as 'note 61, *supra*'.)

non-Christians? There is no doubt that Paul here
is describing a man who not only as sinner does
not do God's will, but at the same time confirms
'according to the inner man' (*eso anthropos*) the
demand of God's Law, and *wants* to carry it out
(verses 15*b*, 18*b*, 19*a*, 21, 22); but he is not in a
position to put it into effect, because sin rules in
his members and forces him to do evil (verses 15*b*,
17, 19*b*, 21*b*, 23). Accordingly, the responsibility
for the action of evil is transferred from the individual and laid on sin (verses 17, 20), or else only the
sarx is made responsible for the action of evil whilst
the *nous* serves God (verses 18*a*, 25*b*). On the one
hand, it is obvious that the capability of assent to
God's will and the intention of carrying out God's
will are to be attributed to the *nous* or *eso anthropos*.
On the other hand, it seems to be assumed that
this man is at most responsible for sin which he has
committed only in the fleshly 'part' of him. Must
we then conclude that here the *nous* does really
seem to stand nearer to God than the *sarx* in other
Pauline statements, that Paul here does seem to
assume a dichotomy in man which he elsewhere
does not recognize?

Against this state of affairs, already pointed out
by myself,[62] it has been urged that the difference

---

[62] *Bekehrung*, pp. 134ff. Two objections have justifiably been
made to my arguments there. R. Bultmann (*Krüger-Festschrift*
[note 59, *supra*], p. 57, note 1; cf. also *Theology*, pp. 212–13
[Ger. pp. 213–14]) declares that the idea criticized by me, that
the mention of the *nous* indicates that man stands under the
claim of God, is fully justified. Althaus ([note 6, *supra*], p. 44)

between Romans 7^{14ff} and the other anthropological
statements of Paul is invalid as Paul is completely
'systematic in his anthropology'.[63] It has also been
suggested that if Romans 7^{14ff} refers to the non-
Christians, it follows that a part of man, the *nous*,
is to be thought of as drawn out of the destruction
of the *sarx*, since the man here portrayed has fallen
prey to sin *only* in so far as he is *sarx*, and that is
only valid for Christians.[64] Moreover, so it is maintained, a distinction between Christian and non-
Christian is alien to Paul. The Christian, like the
non-Christian, must allow that only in the act of
agreeing to it may we believe that God accounts
for us that we are free from Law and sin. Paul has
the Christian as well as the non-Christian in view,
since the Christian is to advance from Romans 7 to
Romans 8; the life of the Christian in accordance
with the spirit (Rom 8^4) 'is life on a different plane
from that of human activity and human belief. It
lies on the level of *God's deed*.'[65] If, according to this

has referred to the fact that not only in Romans 7, but also in
Romans 1 and 2 it is presumed that man *can* assent to the
commands of God, not only that he *should*.

[63] Lekkerkerker (note 61, *supra*), p. 70.

[64] Möller (note 60, *supra*), pp. 14, 24; Lekkerkerker (note 61,
supra), p. 73; also '*Romeinen 7 . . .*', p. 106. Nauck (note 60,
supra) finds in Romans 7 the situation of the believer described,
in so far as he is still 'flesh', and is conscious of the opposition
between *nous* and *sarx*, out of which he can only go forward as
victor. But this is precisely what the man in Romans 7 does
not know.

[65] Lekkerkerker (note 61, *supra*), p. 74; Maurer (note 60,
supra), pp. 46, 52–3, 104. Maurer (p. 46) objects further against

view, in the portrayal of the Christian found in Romans 7[14ff], the gift of *pneuma* is conspicuously absent, this is explained in one of two ways. Either, first, the *nous* in 7[22, 25b] confirms God's Law, which according to 7[14] is *pneumatikos*, with the result that the '*nous* which conforms with it and the personality which through the *nous* serves the *nomos* are indeed *pneumatikos* also'.[66] Or else, secondly, one concludes that the absence of the spirit in Romans 7[14ff] is 'one of the many omissions which often arise in the Pauline letters'.[67]

Althaus, that there can be no New Testament exegesis in a problem such as the interpretation of a passage like Romans 7, 'apart from our own standpoint and our own human prejudices and prejudgements, and that our apparent absence of prejudice is as such also a prejudice'. It is certainly true that an exegesis which designs to determine historically what Paul meant, and which regards such determining as the basic task of exegetical work, obviously takes this intention (namely, to discover as far as possible the *historical* meaning of the text) into consideration as a 'prejudgement'. Again, such exegesis must naturally know the limits which to a certain degree are unavoidably fixed by the historical remoteness of the text and our own point of view clouded by exegetical history. Because of such limits, however, the attempt of exegesis to interpret *historically* cannot be given up as its 'prejudgement'. On the contrary, it is precisely through this method that exegesis will try to remain faithful to its task to hear the word of God in the *historically* determined words of men.

[66] Möller (note 60, *supra*), p. 24. Similarly, Nygren ([note 60, *supra*], pp. 215, 217) speaks simply of the 'spirit', and wrongly names Galatians 5[17] as parallel. The *pneumatikos* is in Romans 7[14] certainly not intended to go with the *ego*! Also Magnusson ([note 60, *supra*], p. 198) speaks of the Christian in Romans 7[14ff] as *sarx* and *pneuma* at the same time.

[67] J. H. Semmelink, quoted by Lekkerkerker (note 61, *supra*), p. 74, note 1.

It is easy to see that in these various attempts to
relate Romans 7[14ff] to Christians, considerable mis-
interpretations of the text have to be made. It is
certainly wrong that Paul here presents the *nous* as
separated from the destruction of the *sarx*, and
neither is it right that the man depicted here is
only as *sarx* a prey to sin, which is something only
true of the Christian. This dualistic anthropology
can, to a certain extent, rightly find support in
some of the previously mentioned statements in
which sin is limited to *sarx* and man has been
absolved of his sin. But the 'dualistic' statements
are within the context of other statements in which
man as a whole being is clearly responsible for his
will and actions,[67a] in which man as a whole being
appears as carnal, sold to sin, and where the *nous*
is just as much a 'function' of the whole sinful man
as the *sarx*, which is termed 'my members'. So 'I
am yet fleshly (*sarkinos*), sold under sin': verses
14*b*, 15, 16, 19, 21, 23, 24; then 'Thus with my
nous I serve the Law of God, but with the *sarx* the
law of sin': verse 25*b*.

The contradiction which the man described here
embodies is not really attributable to 'parts' of the
man, even though the dualistic manner of expression at times gives rise to this impression. Rather,
the desperate situation of this man (verse 24)
results precisely from the fact that he is at the same
time *sarx* and *nous*. And so it is here not a question
of a *nous* free from the destruction of the *sarx*;

[67a] Laeuchli ([note 6, *supra*], p. 21) overlooks this.

and the claim that the Christian is only as *sarx* fallen prey to sin, is, even apart from Romans 7^{14ff}, completely unPauline (cf. texts like Galatians 5^{17}, 2 Corinthians 10^3, and Romans 6^{13}).

But also we must conclude as false both the claims that Paul sees the Christian in the transition from Romans 7 to Romans 8, and also the notion that the Christian's freedom from sin is only valid at the moment when he makes his confession to God's act of declaring him righteous. Paul speaks not only of a *standing* in belief (Rom 5^2, 11^{20}, 1 Cor 15^1, 2 Cor 1^{24}), but also describes the taking away of sin, which takes place in the case of the Christian, as an objective event—certainly not a 'natural' one (Rom 6^{3f}, 6^6, 7^6, 8^2, 1 Cor 6^{11}, etc.). And there is no question in Paul of a *progressive* salvation (cf. only Romans 6^{11-12}).[68] Neither is it right that the Christian's walk in the Spirit does not lie on the plane of human action but on the plane of God's action. Certainly God's action is the root of the Christian's behaviour (Rom 8^2), but this behaviour is then therefore a *reality* in the Christian life, just as much as the sinful behaviour of the non-Christian (Rom 8^4, 1 Thess 4^1, Col 1^4). Paul recognizes, then, a characteristic which differentiates in reality the Christian from the non-Chris-

---

[68] For this reason, it is a quite unjustified inference from the false reference of Romans 7^{14ff} to the Christian, when Maurer ([note 60, *supra*], p. 51) denies the temporal sense of the *nun* in Romans 8^1 and understands this temporal concept in the sense of the eternal act of God which occurred in Christ.

tian, that is, the possession and with it the workings
of the *pneuma*; this *pneuma* is missing from Romans
7^{14ff}, and one cannot introduce it surreptitiously by
declaring the *nous* here as pneumatic or by arbi-
trarily explaining the absence of the *pneuma* as an
omission of the writer's.

From a consideration of Paul's view on the nature of the Christian and the non-Christian man,
it would seem rather that Romans 7^{14ff} can only be
meant as a description of the non-Christian. However, the relative departure of this text from Paul's
other statements about the inner man remains to
be explained. We have already suggested that it
is only Paul's careless and unsystematic dualistic
form of expression which is responsible for the
impression that in some of the statements in this
passage Paul is implying an inner self closer to
God, to be differentiated from the outer man. In
fact, as elsewhere, Paul depicts here the whole
man as subject to sin. Admittedly, it is particularly
emphasized that this man knows of his being lost
in sin, of his doing of evil, and his failure to fulfil
the demand of God's Law.[69] This feature of know-

[69] Bultmann (*Krüger-Festschrift*, note 59, *supra*) disputes that
Paul in Romans 7^{14ff} would have spoken from the point of view
of practical life, and of the fact that the commands of the Law
were impossible to fulfil. Bultmann understands 'the will to do
good' as being 'the trans-subjective tendency of human existence
as a whole', which tends towards 'Life', and the doing of evil
as the trans-subjective gaining of death as the result of such
doing. Similarly, Bultmann (*Theology*, pp. 223–4, 248–9 [Ger.
pp. 223–4, 248–9]), Bornkamm ([note 59, *supra*], pp. 63ff), Fuchs
([note 59, *supra*], pp. 70–1), and Braun ([note 59, *supra*], p. 3).

ing about his own desperate condition is lacking in Romans 1[20ff] and 2[12ff], and because scholars have thought it impossible to concede such a knowledge to the non-Christian, as Paul interprets him, they have always had to relate Romans 7[14ff] to the Christian. That is, as we saw, not possible.

However, it is not difficult to see why Paul speaks here a little differently than elsewhere about the situation of the non-Christian. The section 7[14ff] is not, in the first place, intended primarily to depict the condition of this man but rather has the aim of defending the Law and relieving it from the guilt of sin by showing how man, in accordance with his 'inner man', recognizes, in spite of his evil deeds, the divinity of God's will proclaimed in the Law. If this proof is to convince, however, Paul must also stress man's ability to respond to the command and therefore his confirmation of the Law. A second thing is more important: the non-Christian is seen here consciously and consistently through Christian eyes. Not only is his situation depicted as being completely hopeless, but also the whole description of the non-Christian man is determined by the Christian Spirit-Flesh conflict (Gal 5[17]). Consequently, the opposition between *nous* and *sarx* is more stressed here than elsewhere.

Most important of all, the assent of the 'inner

This, however, contradicts the wording of Romans 7[14ff] completely, as has already been several times pointed out. Cf. G. Schrenk, *ThWb*, II.548, note 25; III.50–1; Gutbrod, pp. 45ff; Althaus, pp. 47ff; and Kuss, pp. 470ff (all note 6, *supra*).

man' to the Law of God does not mean that this 'inner man' is any nearer to God than the corporeal 'members'. Rather, the fact that the inner man recognizes God's commandments as in reality divine and therefore justly obligatory upon him, only serves to underline mankind's desperate situation of being hopelessly lost. Nothing remains but to utter the despairing cry: 'O wretched man that I am. Who will deliver me from the body of this death?' Thus it is precisely in this text, in which man's unconditional assent to God's demands is shown, that he appears before God as sinner *in his whole being*.

Thus we must conclude that the three texts under discussion (Rom 1[20], 2[15], 7[14ff]) confirm our argument that Paul sees the whole man as *sarx* and consequently as sinner.

If we have been correct in seeing man as essentially a sinner because of his nature as *sarx*, and in claiming that his sinfulness cannot be attributed simply to his fleshly and material existence, then one important question remains: How are we to understand the connexion between *sarx* and sin? In many instances, *sarx* appears in Paul as a great power opposing man. Man is '*in* the flesh' (*en sarki*, Gal 2[20], 2 Cor 10[3]), as if he were not himself identical with the *sarx*. The *sarx* has thoughts (*phronema*, Rom 8[6-7]), desires (*epithumia*, Gal 5[16]), mind (*nous*, Col 2[18]), and the Christian is seen between the two conflicting powers *sarx* and *pneuma* (Gal 5[17]). Consequently, it has often been said that for Paul *sarx* is a principle or power governing human kind.[70]

But against this it must be insisted that Paul employs *sarx* and *soma* in the same way for mankind and his actual, human, fleshly existence (cf. I Cor 5^3 with Col 2^5; also Rom 8^{13}, 2 Cor 4$^{10-11}$, 7^5).[71] It is the man who is in the body, it is fleshly, *en sarki* mankind which is governed by sin. The sinfulness of mankind characterized as *sarx* appears in open rebellion against God's will (Rom 8^7), in acting according to one's desire (Gal 5^{16}), in 'boasting' (*kauchasthai*, I Cor 1^{29}, 2 Cor 11^{18}), and in adherence to human and worldly traditions (Col 2$^{18, 23}$). The man characterized by *sarx* is under the *kosmos* and its powers. Thus, Galatians 3^3, 'Are you now perfected in the flesh (*sarki*)?', corresponds to 4^9, 'How can you turn back to the mean and beggarly spirits of the elements?' (*NEB*). *Sarx*

---

[70] Cf. recently among others, J. Kaftan (*Neutestamentliche Theologie* [1927], p. 129), Käsemann ([note 49, *supra*], pp.104–5), Shedd ([note 6, *supra*], pp. 121–2), and Bultmann (*Theology*, pp. 244–5 [Ger. p. 245]); cf. also Kuss ([note 6, *supra*], pp.537–8).

[71] Cf. also Kümmel, *Bekehrung*, pp. 20ff; Gutbrod (note 6, *supra*), pp. 31ff, 40ff, 92ff; E. Schweizer, *ThWb*, VII.131–2. The fact that *sarx* as denoting the sinful man indicates also the concrete man, characterized by body, is plain also from the fact that *mele* can take the place of *sarx* (Rom 7$^{23, 25b}$), and that sin uses the *mele* in order to bring man to death (Rom 6$^{12-13}$, 7^5). Cf. J. Horst, *ThWb*, IV.565–6. The fact that for Paul *soma* and *sarx* can mean the same can be seen also from the expression *soma tes sarkos* (Col 1^{22}, 2^{11}), which was used both for the earthly Jesus and for the past life of the Christian. It also occurs in late Judaism as a description of human, physical man. Cf. Kuhn (note 4, *supra*), p. 107.

denotes the man who lets himself be *determined* by his actual historical existence in the world; it does not describe man in his fundamental nature, but rather in his membership in this passing evil age (Gal 1⁴). In so far as man lets himself be determined by the reality of 'this age' (*aion houtos*), and thereby denotes that he is yet *sarx*, so far is he 'a slave of sin and death' (Rom 6¹⁶).

This connexion of *sarx* and sin, shown in man's historical behaviour, has no exceptions (Rom 3⁹, ²³, 8⁷ᶠᶠ). Moreover, this judgement is not the result of Christian experience, as Paul insists upon the *possibility* that heathens also can be obedient to the commands of the Law. So Romans 2¹⁴⁻¹⁵, ²⁶. This whole point of view is to be seen as Paul's post-conversion judgement upon his own former life as a Torah-righteous Pharisee who since his conversion has learnt to regard his Jewish adherence to the Law as the wrong way to salvation, as indeed, a 'loss' (*zemia*) (Rom 3²⁰, 9³¹, 10³, Phil 3⁷). The common and unavoidable sinfulness of all mankind is not deduced by Paul from his nature as *sarx*, but is, indeed, the necessary consequence of the certainty that only 'in Christ' can God's approval be gained (Rom 3²¹ᶠᶠ, 8⁷⁻¹⁰, Gal 5⁵⁻⁶). Moreover, this sinfulness involving all mankind is something which is only clear to the eyes of faith, looking back upon the past. Only from the Christian point of view is it clear that man is *sarx* in his very existence, and is determined by *sarx* (Rom 7¹⁴, 8⁶⁻⁷).

Paul does not anywhere explain the *source* of

this connexion between man's fleshly and sinful existence. On one occasion only he says that sin began with Adam: 'It was through one man that sin entered the world, and through sin death, and thus death pervaded the whole human race, inasmuch as all men have sinned' (Rom 5^{12}, *NEB*). The exact meaning of this text is still debated, but it is scarcely debatable that Paul here expresses two views side by side which cannot immediately be reconciled: 'Through the sin of the first man, sin and its consequence death, entered the world' and 'death has come to all men, *because* all have sinned.'[72] Paul does not here maintain that each

[72] This admittedly depends upon the translation of *eph hō* in Romans 5^{12} by 'because'. This translation dates back to the Peschitta (*behai de*), and was followed by all Reformers from Erasmus onwards: cf. R. Pfister, *Das Problem der Erbsünde bei Zwingli* (Diss. Zürich, 1938), p. 106. Today, it is the customary translation: cf. e.g. Bultmann, *ThWb*, III.15, note 69; M. Dibelius, '*Vier Worte des Römerbriefs*', *Symbolae Biblicae Upsalienses*, III.(1944).7; Gaugler (note 59, *supra*), p. 127; S. Hanson, 'The Unity of the Church in the New Testament', *Acta Seminarii Neotestamentici Upsaliensis*, XIV.(1946).65; G. Lindeskog, *Studien zum neutestamentlichen Schöpfungsgedanken*, I.(Uppsala Universitets Arsskrift [1952], XI).221; Barrett (note 59, *supra*), p. 111; Bauer (note 19, *supra*), p. 569; O. Kuss, *Der Römerbrief*, Part I.(1957).231. This translation corresponds to the word usage of Paul (2 Cor 5^4, Phil 3^{12}, 4^{10}). It has been attacked since the concluding words (5^{12d}), 'since all have sinned', appear as a troublesome side idea, and *eph ho* is taken in a relative sense, in relation to *ho thanatos*. In this case, it either means in the sense of *origin* 'on grounds of which all sinned' (so Pfister, pp. 107–8; Schlier [note 5, *supra*], p. 26; Galling [note 5, *supra*], p. 16; J. Leipoldt, *Der Tod bei Griechen und Juden* [1942], pp. 61–2); or else in the sense of *end* ('*c'est pour récolter la mort*'—J. Héring, *Le royaume de Dieu et sa venue*,

man has by his birth inherited Adam's sin,[73] but
only that it is since Adam's sin to be found in every
man, and that in consequence of the sin of each
man, all men die. But he puts beside that the statement that each man merits his own death because
of his own sin—death which since Adam has been
the punishment for sin. This thought about each individual's responsibility for his own death cannot

[1937], p. 157; similarly Stauffer, *Theologie* [note 59, *supra*],
p. 248, note 176, ET, p. 270, note 176). However, there are
objections to both translations. The first contradicts Romans
6[23], where death is the *result* of sin. The second implies that
ho thanatos in 5[12d] would mean, contrary to the related word in
5[12c], the death of the individual man, and that then the death in
5[12c], otherwise than in 5[12a, b], would not be the consequence, but
the end of sin. That Paul in 5[12] is partly dependent upon the
wording of Wisdom of Solomon 2[23-4], 'God created man for
immortality' (*ep' aphtharsia*), is quite unproven, since Paul is
here dependent upon the late Judaistic teaching on sin in general
(against Stauffer, loc. cit.).

[73] So again Schaefer ([note 5, *supra*], pp. 29, 35) and Gutbrod
([note 6, *supra*], p. 140). Also H. Lietzmann (*An die Römer* [4th
edn, 1933], p. 61) states wrongly that 'the teaching on original
sin of the early Church would presumably appear as the corresponding hypothesis to that of Paul'. S. Lyonnet (see Huby [note
59, *supra*], pp. 532ff) and G. Lafont ('*Sur l'interprétation de
Romains 5.15-21*', *Recherches de Science Religieuse*, XLV.[1957].
481ff) translate *eph ho* by 'in so far as', and thus understand the
individual's sin as a secondary cause of the eternal damnation
of all men, beside the primary cause which is the sin of Adam.
Similarly, probably, Barth (*Christus und Adam* [note 6a, *supra*],
pp. 10, 33). But this is quite arbitrary. Kuss ([note 72, *supra*],
p. 231) finds the first mention of original sin in 5[19]. J. Blinzler
(art. '*Erbsünde*', *LThK*, III.[1959].966-7) leaves this question
open. Bultmann (*Theology I*, p. 251 [Ger. pp. 251-2]) thinks
Paul's notion of original sin derives from Gnostic myths, but is
then obliged to describe 5[12d] as 'unclear'.

be described or dismissed as an unfortunate notion of secondary importance.[74] On the contrary, for Paul it is most important, because only by retaining this idea of personal responsibility does man appear as guilty of his own death (cf. Rom 6[20-1, 23]). Moreover, Paul is only following Jewish tradition in placing side by side inherited death as a result of common sinfulness and man's own responsibility for his death as a result of his sin.[75] From the fact that Paul has not tried to find any logical

[74] According to Lietzmann (note 73, *supra*), 5[12d] is 'a troublesome rather than helpful sidetrack'. Similarly, Bultmann, *ZNW*, L.(1959).154. Gaugler ([note 72, *supra*], pp. 127ff) thinks that to understand 5[12d] as an expression of the personal answerability of the individual contradicts the tenor of Paul's thought, but he does not mention the sentence in his explanation. S. Hanson ([note 72, *supra*], pp. 66ff) sets aside the thought that each individual brings on his own death through his sin, by understanding Adam in Romans 5[12] as a collective personality, so that Paul in the same way could say that Adam sinned or that mankind as a whole sinned: 'From the aspect of representation, the individual and the collective body are identical.' R. P. Shedd ([note 6, *supra*], p. 108) interprets the connexion between the sin of Adam and that of all mankind by saying that 'in Adam' all already sinned—so also Nygren ([note 60, *supra*], p. 159) and Davies ([note 44, *supra*], p. 32). But Paul says only that in Adam all mankind *dies* (1 Cor 15[22]). In spite of the notion of Adam as a 'comprehensive personality', it is not possible to ground the Pauline assumption of the common sinfulness of mankind in its belonging to 'the first man'. Dodd ([note 59, *supra*], pp. 78–9) also is wrong on this point, though not mentioning the meaning of 5[12d]. Leenhardt ([note 59, *supra*], pp. 83–4) is unclear.

[75] See the references in W. Bousset, *Die Religion des Judentums im späthellenistischen Zeitalter* (3rd edn, ed. H. Gressmann, 1926), pp. 406ff; G. F. Moore, *Judaism in the First Centuries of the Christian Era*, I.(1927).474ff; Shedd (note 6, *supra*), pp. 80ff; H. J. Schoeps, *Paulus* (1959), pp. 197ff.

compromise between these two important claims
about the universality of sin and therefore of death
on the one hand and the individual's responsibility
for his death by reason of his sin on the other hand,
it can be concluded that in Romans 5^{12} Paul speaks
about the beginning of sin and hence of death, but
is not particularly interested in this beginning;
rather it is the *universality* of sin and death which
interests him and which he wants to contrast with
the universality of the life given in Christ.[76] The
reference to Adam is not intended to *explain* the
origin of sin or pardon man for his sinfulness, but
only to emphasize, by referring to its historical
beginnings, the universality of sin and, with it,
death which Christian faith substantiates.

Paul, therefore, does not intend to derive man's
common sinfulness and hence his liability to death
from his life in the flesh, or from his descendance
from a common father of the race, but rather, is
merely concerned to establish this universality of
sin and death as a historical fact.[77] Much more,
he sets its source in the actual behaviour of the
individual who violates God's will and therefore
is liable to death.[78] And so, like Jesus, Paul sees

[76] So rightly Dibelius (note 72, *supra*), pp. 7–8; similarly Dodd
(note 59, *supra*), p. 80.

[77] E. Stauffer (*Theology* [note 59, *supra*], p. 68 [Ger. p. 52])
distinguishes the thought of historical heredity from that of
biological heredity, and denotes only the first as biblical.

[78] Paul Althaus ('*Das Bild Gottes bei Paulus*', ThBl, XX.
[1941].81ff) has from this concluded that Paul can also simply
base man's liability to death in his belonging to the first Adam

man exclusively from the point of view of his relation to God and therefore judges man as being hostile to Him and lost in the *kosmos*. Paul con-

---

as the beginner of the first generation of men (Rom $5^{15, 17}$, 1 Cor $15^{22, 45}$). According to Althaus, this fact must be seen in connexion with Paul's occasional teaching that the image of God in man is lacking in natural man as man, and is first given to Christians through being made like Christ, who is the image of God. This is based on Colossians 3^{10}, 1 Corinthians 15^{45}. However, according to Althaus, Paul also says that man lost the image of God through sin (Rom 3^{23}), so that he must have originally possessed it. And this corresponds with Romans 5^{12}, which states that man's fall into sin and thus into death originated in the deed of Adam. Now, it is doubtless correct, that in Paul the two representations of death as the sign of Adamic mankind and as the consequence of Adam's sin occur side by side. Certainly, Paul did not notice any contradiction between them. His only interest in the idea of the original liability to death of Adamic mankind was that it served to emphasize the universality of death, which itself in Romans 6^{23} is not simply a fact of creation, but can be an unavoidable *consequence* of sin. However, Althaus is hardly right when he disputes that there is any connexion between the idea of an image of God originally possessed but lost through the Fall on the one hand, and the idea of the image of God given to man through Christ on the other—and all this merely because Paul does not speak of the *renewing* of the *lost* image of God through Christ (so also S. V. McCasland, *JBL*, LXIX.[1950].99). For despite Althaus, in Colossians 3^{10}, 'Having put on the new (man), which is renewed into knowledge (of God) according to the image of its Creator', the Creator (*tou ktisantos auton*) doubtless relates, from Paul's customary use of *ktizo* (Rom 1^{25}, 1 Cor 11^9, Col 1^{16}), to the first creation of mankind. So also Jervell (note 18*a*, *supra*, p. 250). The meaning of the sentence is thus that the Christian is renewed through becoming like the New Man, Christ; and that through this at the same time a likening to the image of the Creator also takes place. So E. Lohmeyer, *Die Briefe an die Philipper, an die Kolosser, an Philemon* (1930), pp. 140ff; Werner

nects this fact of man's remoteness from God with his existence as *sarx*. This is a use of terms, capable of misunderstanding, which can at best

Bieder, *Der Kolosserbrief* (1943), pp. 197–8; G. Kittel, *ThWb*, II.395. If Paul does not actually clearly state that the image of God given through belonging to the 'New Man', Christ, is a *renewing* of the lost, original image of God, one must nevertheless draw this conclusion. And F. W. Eltester (*Eikon im Neuen Testament* [1958], p. 163) has not brought any decisive objection to this—and in particular has not shown that *ktizo* in Colossians 3[10] denotes the new creation. Paul has thus described the unavoidability of death in two not fully identical ways, and has seen the image of God in man as a reality, which was lost to all men at the Fall in sin, and is first given again through Christ. So E. Käsemann, '*Eine urchristliche Taufliturgie*', *Festschrift R. Bultmann* (1949), p. 138 = *Exegetische Versuche und Besinnungen*, I.(1960).41; E. Lohse, '*Imago Dei bei Paulus*', *Libertas Christiana: Festschrift für F. Delekat* (1957), p. 133; J. Jervell (note 18*a*, *supra*), pp. 179–80, 232, 286–7. P. I. Bratsiotis (note 5, *supra*, p. 33) wrongly states that man has not quite lost the image of God. K. L. Schmidt ('*Homo imago Dei im Alten und Neuen Testament*', *Eranos-Jahrbuch* [1947–8], pp. 192ff) has also made clear that in Romans 1[22-3] it is presupposed that man has 'forfeited the title "image of God" which belongs to him'. Similarly, Morna D. Hooker, 'Adam in Romans I', *NTSt*, VI.(1959–60). 305; J. Jervell (note 18*a*, *supra*), pp. 312ff. Finally, Paul uses the idea of the image of God in 1 Corinthians 11[7] for the man (male) alone. Whatever this as yet unclarified thought may mean in detail, it certainly does not in any sense describe mankind as a whole, or its standing before God, but merely illustrates in some way the position of the man as over against the woman. J. Jervell (note 18*a*, *supra*, pp. 292ff) also remarks that 1 Corinthians 11[7] is an isolated text in the Pauline tradition, and is irreconcilable with the other interpretations of Genesis 1[27]. Jervell's attempt to claim that the questioning of the image of God in the case of women is an idea which Paul has taken over from Judaistic exegesis, is possible. But it shows, at any rate, that the expression is not yet really understood by us.

be explained with A. Schlatter[79] by saying that Paul contrasts man with God as the bearer of the Spirit: 'the *Spirit* is the mark of God and the Agent of His activity. Flesh, on the other hand, is the mark of man in all his dissimilarity from God.' Nevertheless, in whatever way the origin of this terminology is to be explained, it is clear that man, for Paul, is a historical being who derives his nature from his existence as a member of the present evil age, and from his living in accordance with this historical existence.

Paul thus differs from Jesus in his view of man inasmuch as his use of Rabbinical and Hellenistic terminology often leads him into a word-usage which is not always unambiguous. However, the main lines of Paul's picture are in accord with that of Jesus. Consequently, for Paul also salvation is not a natural or human solution to man's problems, but a historical action of God, involving the beginning of the new age and empowering man to a new way of life by transferring him 'into the Kingdom of His beloved Son' (Col 1[13]). The picture of man in the teaching of Paul is like that of Jesus not an *a priori* presupposition, but has

[79] (Note 49, *supra*), p. 272. Cf. also E. Käsemann (note 49, *supra*), pp. 112, 116: 'Flesh is the *worldlikeness* of mankind. Just as the Pauline "metaphysic" of being in the flesh is to be understood from the constant historical fact of Existence as it already is in the world, so also Paul's "metaphysic" of sin is to be understood from the historical fact of constant temptation in the world, and also from the constant and manifest sin which is historically and empirically, if not logically, bound to it.'

been formed retrospectively, out of his own experience of present salvation, but using concepts
and doctrines which he brought with him from
his own background as a Hellenistic Jew. Thus,
Paul's view of man distinguishes itself completely
from every purely humanistic or descriptive view
of man, as much as from every idealistic or dualistic conception.[80]

[80] So R. Bultmann, *ThLZ* (1927), p. 35: 'Pauline anthropology
is drawn from the point of view of the justified, and is thus itself
as a statement an act of the new life, and not an anthropology in
a general or obvious sense.'

FOUR

Johannine Theology

IS NOT THE view of the Johannine Gospel and Epistles distinctive and at odds with that expressed in different ways by Jesus and Paul?[81] To this question we must now turn.

John does indeed say that man is 'from beneath (*ek tōn katō*)', 'of this kosmos' (Jn 8[23]), and stresses that 'that which is born of the flesh is flesh and that which is born of the Spirit is spirit' (Jn 3[6]), that 'unless one is born of water and of the Spirit, he cannot enter into the Kingdom of God' (Jn 3[5]).

---

[81] The thesis that the Book of Revelation was written by the same author as the Gospel and Epistles of John, and, indeed, comprises a necessary filling-out of the theology of the Gospel, has been recently put forward again from a variety of grounds. Cf. E. Lohmeyer, *Die Offenbarung des Johannes* (1926 = 2nd edn, 1953), pp. 198–9; P. Feine and J. Behm, *Einleitung in das Neue Testament* (9th edn, 1950), pp. 279ff; H. Preisker, *ThBl*, XV.(1936).185ff; Stauffer, *Theology* (note 59, *supra*), pp. 28, 40–1 (Ger. pp. 13, 25–6); Ph. H. Menoud, *L'Évangile de Jean d'après les recherches récentes* (2nd edn, 1947), pp. 73ff; M. Albertz, *Die Botschaft des Neuen Testaments*, I.2.(1952).347ff; Philip Carrington, *The Early Christian Church*, I.(1957).363; F.-M. Braun, *Jean le théologien et son évangile dans l'Église ancienne* (1959), pp. 43ff; with hesitations also W. Michaelis, *Einleitung in das Neue Testament* (2nd edn, 1954), pp. 312ff. But the word-usage and the theological perspectives show Revelation to be the work of a quite different spirit. We shall consequently count it among the other sub-apostolic writings.

Does this imply that the man who is 'dust of the earth with base and ungodly desires' 'stands so far from the life-giving Spirit (Jn 6⁶³), and hence from the Kingdom of God which, like God Himself (Jn 4²⁴), is "of the Spirit" (Jn 3⁵), that he is shut out from God by his very earthly existence'?[82] Is mankind as seen by John therefore inextricably bound in an antithesis between this material world and a spiritual higher world?

If this is correct, then we would have to assume that John took for granted an inner dualism in man, or at very least, a special inherent nearness to God in his inner man. But that is not the case. The few descriptions of the inner man do not stand in opposition to those concerning the outer man, and emphasize its distance from God rather than any natural nearness to God.[83] John does not see man bound in an inextricable opposition to God, and so it can be concluded that he does not recognize any *metaphysical* dualism between man and

[82] H. J. Holtzmann (note 9, *supra*), II.520.

[83] *Kardia* occurs more frequently—John 12⁴⁰, 13², 14¹, ²⁷, 16⁶, ²², 1 John 3¹⁹⁻²⁰—and always to describe man as far from God, excepting 16²², where the eschatological joy is the subject. *Psuche* usually denotes life (Jn 12²⁵, 13³⁷, 15¹³, 1 Jn 3¹⁶), only twice, and then unaccented, the inner part of man, without any opposition to the outer man (Jn 10²⁴, 3 Jn 2). *Splagchna* occurs singly and without particular significance in 1 John 3¹⁷. In 1 John 5²⁰, *dianoia* is used of 'the understanding given us to know the truth', the possibility of knowing which has been awakened in the Christian through the Son (see J. Behm, *ThWb*, IV.[1942]. 964–5). In John 6⁶³, *pneuma* in opposition to *sarx* denotes the divine spirit.

God. Certainly, man for John as for Jesus and Paul always stands over against God, and from this he derives his characteristic stamp. This is clear from his use of the terms *anthropos* and *sarx*.[84]

Nevertheless, the opposition of man to God is not based upon his essential *nature* as opposed to God. Rather, *sarx* is man as he is, unrenewed by the divine *pneuma*, and such a man is characterized by the fact that he is living *en kosmo* and demonstrates by manifesting the passions of the *sarx* that he is *ek tou kosmou* (1 Jn 2[16]). This is the concept which is most characteristic of man in John's view. *Kosmos*[85] occurs very frequently in John, and sometimes simply describes God's world as creation (Jn 1[9], 17[5], 1 Jn 4[1], etc.), but it can also denote the totality of mankind, towards which

---

[84] *Anthropos* usually occurs without emphasis as the description of man in his given state (e.g. Jn 1[4, 9], 2[25], 7[22-3], 8[17], 11[50], 16[21], 17[6], 18[17], 19[5]). It can also mean man as standing over against God, and differentiated from God (Jn 3[27], 5[34, 41], 10[33], 12[43], 1 Jn 5[9]), or, indeed, as sinner before God (Jn 3[19], 9[16b, 24]). *Sarx* is used by John mainly for the human existence of the earthly Jesus (Jn 1[14], 6[51-6], 1 Jn 4[2], 2 Jn 7). In a few other cases, the opposition to God or God's Spirit is strongly emphasized (Jn 3[6], 6[63], 8[15], 1 Jn 2[16]). Only in John 17[2] does *pasa sarx*, 'all flesh', indicate simply mankind—the Old Testament usage. *Soma* is used only for the body of the crucified Christ (Jn 2[21], 19[31], 20[12]).

[85] For the Johannine *Kosmos* concept, cf. Friedrich Büchsel, *Johannes und der hellenistische Synkretismus* (1928), pp. 101ff; H. Odeberg, *The Fourth Gospel* (1929), pp. 115ff; E. Percy, *Untersuchungen über den Ursprung der johanneischen Theologie*, (Diss., Lund 1939), pp. 125ff; and particularly Bultmann, *G.u.V.*, I.(1933).135ff; also *Theology*, II.50ff (Ger. pp. 367ff).

God's redeeming activity is directed (Jn 1^{29}, 3^{16}, 8^{26}, 1 Jn 2^2, etc.). This human world is denoted as *ho kosmos houtos*, which is occasionally put as the opposite of the world to come. So John 12^{25}: 'He who hates his life in this world will keep it for eternal life' (cf. also 1 Jn 4^{17}, 2^{17}). But in most cases this 'coming world' is described as the 'higher world'. So John 8^{23}: 'He said to them, You are from below, I am from above. You are of this world, I am not of this world' (cf. also 12^{31-2}, 13^1, 18^{36}, 1 Jn 4^{3ff}).[86]

The predominance of this special concept of the two worlds shows that John has not simply taken over his *kosmos*-concept from early Christianity. Paul means by *ho kosmos houtos* the present world history, parallel to *ho aion houtos* (1 Cor 1^{20}, 3^{19}, 5^{10}, 7^{31}), but here the point of contrast is always the *coming* age, as in later Judaism. When John uses *kosmos* he turns the concept into a *spatial* one, and though the term 'this world' corresponds to the usage of later Judaism, the content actually denoted is derived from Gnosticism.[87] Such Gnostic-naturalistic understanding of *kosmos* as a whole entity of existence opposed to God seems to be suggested by other descriptions of this 'lower world'. It is the world of darkness (Jn 3^{19}, 8^{12}, 12^{46}), it is antagonistic towards God (Jn $15^{18, \ 24}$, $17^{9, \ 25}$),

[86] The opposite intended to 'this world' in John 9^{39}, 11^9, 16^{11}, is not certain.

[87] Cf. references in Odeberg (note 85, *supra*), pp. 123ff; W. Bauer, *Das Johannesevangelium* (3rd edn, 1933), pp. 19–20; H. Jonas, *Gnosis und spätantiker Geist*, I.(1934).146ff.

and ruled by Satan (Jn 12[31], 14[30], 16[11], 1 Jn 5[19]).[88] The Jews are the classic opponents of the 'One who has been sent' and the typical representatives of the godless state of the world. In John 8[22-3] they are accused of being 'from below, of this world'. It is said of them: 'You are of your father the devil' (Jn 8[44]). Similarly, everyone who sins is in the power of the devil, just as Cain, who killed his brother, is 'of the evil one' (1 Jn 3[8, 12]).

It almost appears as if man's very *existence* in the *kosmos* is the cause of his remoteness from and antagonism to God. However, the plea of the High-Priestly prayer, 'I do not pray that thou shouldst take them out of the world, but that thou shouldst keep them from the evil' (Jn 17[15]), militates against such a naturalistic view of the Johannine *kosmos*-concept. Here we seem to have a clear parallel to Paul's *sarx*-concept, since living in the world does not *necessarily* involve servitude to Satan, and hence sinful separation from God. This is confirmed by closer examination. Sin does not consist simply in being *in* (*en*) the world, which even applies to the 'One who is sent' and those with Him (Jn 13[1], 17[11], 1 Jn 4[17]). Sin consists rather in being of (*ek*) the world, or of the earth (*ek tes ges*), which corresponds to being 'not of God', *ek theou ouk einai* (Jn 3[31], 8[23, 47], 15[19], 17[14, 16],

---

[88] John 5[19], 'The whole world lies in (the power of) the evil', in view of 5[18] doubtless refers to Satan, in whose power the world lies. Cf. W. Bauer (note 19, *supra*), pp. 710, 1153 (ET, pp. 447, 697-8); F. Büchsel, *Die Johannesbriefe* (1933), p. 88; R. Schnackenburg, *Die Johannesbriefe* (1953), p. 259.

18³⁶, 1 Jn 2¹⁶, 4⁵⁻⁶). This expression, *einai ek*, is characteristic for John.[89] Basically it is a term denoting origin (cf. John 8⁴⁴), but it is used in describing man not according to his nature, but according to his actions. The 'being of the earth' shows itself in 'speaking of the earth' (Jn 3³¹), the 'being of the *kosmos*' in 'speaking of the *kosmos*' (Jn 4⁵). The 'being from below' leads to 'death in sins' (Jn 8²³⁻⁴), the 'being of the devil' shows itself in the deed of sin (1 Jn 3⁸). This behaviour of man 'of the world' is not a consequence of his inherent nature, as John 3⁶, 'that which is born of the flesh is flesh', might imply. For, on the one hand it is taken for granted that the *kosmos* cannot receive the divine Spirit and does not receive the One Sent (Jn 14¹⁷, 17²⁵). On the other hand, the believers are 'in the *kosmos*' (Jn 17¹¹), but are hated by the world because they are not 'of the world' (Jn 15¹⁹). The believers are born, it is true, with the desires of the flesh and of humanity (Jn 1¹³ᵃ), but through belief they are born again (Jn 1¹³ᵇ, 1 Jn 3⁹), and their status as believers protects them from death (Jn 8²⁴), and consequently, from perdition (Jn 3¹⁶).

Man's nature as antagonistic to God, therefore,

---

[89] Cf. on this R. Bultmann, *Das Evangelium des Johannes* (10th edn, 1941 = 16th edn, 1959), p. 97, note 3; p. 117, note 6; also his *Theology*, II.60–1 (Ger., pp. 375–6); Schnackenburg (note 88, *supra*), pp. 114, 199. The word-usage here, as with Paul's use of *sarx* (note 48, *supra*), is admittedly not quite uniform, since *en to kosmo* in 1 John 2¹⁵⁻¹⁶ denotes the *kosmos* at enmity with God.

is not due to his constitutional make-up, but to his sinful actions. John also presupposes that all men are in sin (Jn 7^{19}, 9^{34}, 16^8, 1 Jn $1^{8, 10}$), which their subjugation to the power of sin demonstrates. So John 8^{34}: 'Everyone who commits sin is a slave of sin.' This submission to sin, manifesting itself in sinful acts (Jn 3^{19}, $8^{24, 34a}$, 1 Jn 3^4), is, however, the specific fault of individual men as it is not a question of an inherent and unavoidable fate (Jn $3^{19, 36}$, 9^{41}). The results of the guilt of man are his liability to death (8^{21-4}), his being under God's wrath and his rejection by God's judgement (Jn $3^{16, 36}$, $5^{24, 29}$, 9^{41}). The most outstanding instance of the sinful behaviour of the man who lives *ek tou kosmou* is his refusal of obedience to the revelation of God in Christ (Jn 8^{24}, 9^{41}, 15^{22ff}, 16^9, 1 Jn 4^3). The rejection of Jesus denotes man's attempt to set himself up against God, to assert himself. So John 5^{44ff}, 'How can you believe, who receive glory from one another?' In this condition of self-assertion, of being *ek tou kosmou*, of being in sin, man can find out something about his present nature, but nothing about his nature as it should be according to God's intention. For man is created by God and ought to know that as a created being he should live in conformity to the Creator (Jn $1^{3-4, 10-11}$, 3^{27}).[90] Man, however,

[90] Cf. Bultmann (note 89, *supra*), p. 25: 'For man, the decisive understanding of himself should have been the consciousness of his createdness. Merely in such knowledge he should have been "in the light", and therefore have had life in the sense in which created man . . . can have life.'

denies this knowledge by setting himself up as
his own authority, and submits himself to the
ruler of this world, and allows himself to be dictated to by him (Jn 1[10]: 'the world knew Him not',
8[41ff]).[91]

For John, too, therefore, man stands in God's
history between Creation and Judgement, living
in a world hastening to its end (Jn 12[25], 16[4], 1 Jn
2[18]). He is characterized by his existence determined by the Lord of this world and consequently
lives in sin. John does not say how man has
arrived at this state. He does not argue that the
sin of the first man is responsible for it. He is
only concerned with the fact of man's remoteness
from God, not with its origin.[92] The important
thing is that man in so far as he finds himself in
history lets himself be dictated to by the world
and therefore is lost in sin and isolation from God.
Only a deed on God's part can free him from this
isolation. And this deed of God does not need to
divest man of his worldly existence determined by
nature, but aims at translating him into a new
historical worldly existence determined by *history*.
This new historical existence, communicated to

[91] Cf. Bultmann (note 89, *supra*), pp. 33–4: The world of
mankind 'has made itself self-sufficient as a *kosmos* over against
God. It does not wish to understand itself from being the
Creation of God, and can only understand itself from itself. In
this, therefore, consists the Johannine dualism between God and
world, between light and darkness.'
[92] So rightly Schlatter (note 49, *supra*), p. 172. Cf. also
Bultmann (note 89, *supra*), p. 28.

man by believing in the 'One Sent', is shown in the gift of Sonship to God which has now become possible through His mission (Jn 1[12], 1 Jn 3[2a]), and in man's living in hope in the present age, the age between Christ's conquest of the world and its ruler and the promised new Creation (Jn 3[14-15], 12[31], 6[40], 16[33], 1 Jn 3[2b]). John too sees man as a *historical* being in the midst of this passing age. His dualism of man-world and God is historical, not natural and timeless.[93]

[93] See Schlatter (note 49, *supra*), p. 172: 'Not a single sentence of John employs naturalistic categories. On the contrary, it is ethical categories which are used when the opposition is at its sharpest, and it is precisely these categories which, according to John, give to the antithesis against the world its uncompromisable severity.' Cf. further E. Gaugler, '*Das Christuszeugnis des Johannesevangeliums*', in *Jesus Christus im Zeugnis der Heiligen Schrift und der Kirche* (1936), p. 53: 'The Johannine dualism is not cosmological, but historical. The world is not evil, because it is material. . . . It is "darkness" (*skotia*) inasmuch as it has alienated itself from its dependence upon God, and not in itself.' Also Bultmann insists: 'Existence in the world (that is, "out of" the world) is thought of as a "How" of human existence. The existence of man is world-existence. . . . The world-existence of men . . . is no situation of nature, but an existence determined by his state—the state of a man being delivered up' (note 85, *supra*, p. 138—cf. also quotation in note 91, *supra*). However, Bultmann claims not only that the necessary 'demythologization' of the New Testament must eliminate the thought of Creation and of eschatological fulfilment in time by exposing their understanding of existence (*Offenbarung und Heilsgeschehen* [1941], pp. 27ff, esp. pp. 31, 45, 60 = *Kerygma and Myth*, ed. H. W. Bartsch [ET 1952], pp. 1ff, esp. pp. 3-4, 20-1, 40 [Ger. 1948], pp. 15ff, esp. pp. 18, 32, 44), but has also hazarded the exegetical interpretation, that John did not mean either the Creation 'in the beginning' or the judgement and resurrection in a temporal sense. So his John Commentary

It cannot be disputed that John uses here dualistic terminology which is partly Gnostic in origin, which like Paul's anthropological terminology, is liable to be misunderstood. Nevertheless, it is also clear that John had neither a preconceived nor an elaborated dualistic concept of man nor any philosophical concept of man's natural essence. Again, John's picture of man is not simply the result of the taking over of Hellenistic ideas. Rather, John has *a posteriori* based his view of man upon the experience of God's historical act of salvation in Christ. This view of man, like that of Jesus and Paul, can only be understood from the standpoint of faith in God's historical act of salvation.

(note 89, *supra*), pp. 15, 18, 20–1, 379 note 6, 193–4, 196–7, 162, 262 note 7, 465 note 1. Cf. also his *Theology*, II.80 (Ger. p. 391). But in order to achieve this, Bultmann must not only dispute the clearly temporal character of such expressions as 'beginning', 'before the *kosmos* was', and 'foundation of the *kosmos*' in John 1¹, 17⁵, ²⁴, but also is obliged to negate the temporal eschatological expressions in John 5²⁸⁻⁹, 6³⁹⁻⁴⁰, ⁴⁴, ⁵⁴ and 12⁴⁸, and to explain 'I will come again' in John 14³ in an individualistic sense. All this will not do. The temporal expressions about creation and fulfilment are quite indispensable. Consequently, Bultmann presents a fissiparious picture of man according to John, since he indeed excludes all natural interpretations of man's existence, but at the same time does not speak of any real historical standing which man occupies in God's *Heilsgeschichte* between Creation and Parousia. Similarly, Bultmann talks of the understanding of man in the New Testament as a whole (*G.u.V.*, II.59ff), and says that the actual life of man 'plays itself out rather in the momentary, the individual, in the sphere of history' (p. 73). But this history is not the unrecallable march of events leading on to the end of time, in whose course God's dealings in salvation began at a particular time and led on to a particular temporal fulfilment. On the contrary, 'history' is 'every meeting-point in the Now, through which I am asked, whether I will deliver myself up, and thus open myself for the Future which conceals itself in the meeting-point in the Now' (p. 71). In this way, the *recurring* 'moment of decision' takes the place of the definiteness of the *once-for-all* historical action of God. For criticism of Bultmann's elimination of John's temporal eschatology, cf. W. G. Kümmel, *Die Eschatologie der Evangelien* (1936), pp. 21ff; and on his removal of the linear concept of time from the New Testament as a whole, W. G. Kümmel, '*Mythische Rede und Heilsgeschehen im Neuen Testament*', *Kerygma und Mythos*, II.(1952).153ff = *Conjectanea Neotestamentica*, XI.(1948).109ff.

FIVE

The Other Writings
of the New Testament

OUR EXAMINATION of the view of man in Jesus, Paul and John has shown us that, in spite of differences in terminology and a certain variety in their individual emphases, all three central forms of the New Testament proclamation presuppose essentially the same conception of man. Man is seen solely as the one who stands before God. He is created by God and is in duty bound in obedience to his Creator. He tries to set himself up against God and thus becomes a sinner in the sight of God. His sin does not have root in his natural bodily existence. Rather, man is essentially a *unity*, whose whole being stands over against God and is therefore ripe for His final judgement. Only God's sending of Jesus Christ has given him the possibility of salvation from the condemnation which awaits him. This picture of man within history is the outcome of a judgement of faith, of belief in the historical act of salvation by God in Christ, and can therefore only really be understood and affirmed through such a judgement of faith.

The few references to man in the remaining writings of the New Testament accord with this general picture. The presupposition of every form of proclamation is the fact that all men are sinners, and therefore need forgiveness from God.[94] This common sinfulness of man does not depend upon man's entanglement by material things, as inner and outer man are equally sinful: 'We all once walked in the passions of our flesh, following the desires of body and mind' (Eph 2[3]; cf. Eph 4[17–18], Tit 1[15], Heb 10[22], 1 Pet 3[21]).[95] Rather do all men

---

[94] Acts 2[38], 3[19, 26], 5[31], 10[43], 13[38], 26[18], Ephesians 2[1], Hebrews 1[3], 2[17], 5[9], 7[26–7], James 1[14], 1 Peter 2[24], 2 Peter 1[9], Revelation 1[5].

[95] On the correct meaning of Ephesians 2[3], cf. E. Percy (note 59, *supra*), pp. 261–2; E. Schweizer, *ZNW*, XLVIII.(1957). 252–3; H. Schlier, *Der Brief an die Epheser* (1957), p. 107. In 1 Peter 2[11], 'Dear friends, I beg you, as aliens in a foreign land, to abstain from the lusts of the flesh, which war against the soul', it seems clear that 'the world of matter, of which natural man is formed', stands over against 'the immortal soul, the spiritual and divine part in man'. So R. Knopf, *Die Briefe Petri und Judä* (1912), pp. 101–2; similarly G. Wohlenberg, *Der 1. und 2. Petrusbrief und der Judasbrief* (3rd edn, 1923), pp. 67–8; F. Hauck, *Die katholischen Briefe* (1933), p. 53; E. G. Selwyn, *The First Epistle of Peter* (1949), pp. 169–70; E. Schweizer, *ZNW*, XLVIII.(1957).251, also *ThWb*, VII.145. This interpretation, which would imply a dualism in man in 1 Peter, could find support in the fact that in 1 Peter *psuche* denotes the justified man (1[9, 22], 2[25], 4[19]). But against this, it must be insisted that these texts do not suggest any opposition between outer and inner man. Moreover, in 1 Peter 3[18], 4[1–2], and particularly 4[6], *sarx* denotes the *whole* earthly man (on 4[6], cf. E. Schweizer, *ThWb*, VI.446). Apart from these considerations, H. Windisch (*Die katholischen Briefe* [3rd edn, 1951], pp. 61–2) makes quite clear that in the Fourth Book of Maccabees in a similar way, both *soma* and *psuche* are equally subjected to the lusts and set over against the *logismos*, which conquers these lusts. The singular expression in 1 Peter 2[11] thus does not imply an inner dualism in man between body and soul, but deals with the battle of the lusts which enslave man to the world against the

belong to this present evil age (2 Tim 4[10], Tit 2[12]) in the service of the Ruler of this age (Eph 2[1], 6[12], Heb 2[14]), and are thereby liable to death (Acts 11[18], Eph 2[1, 5], Heb 2[14–15]). Man, immersed in the present world, is in every way different from and separate from God (Acts 5[4], 14[15], Heb 6[16–17], 7[8], 8[2], 1 Pet 4[2], 2 Pet 1[21]), and is rushing hopelessly towards the imminent judgement of God (Heb 6[2], Jas 5[9], 2 Pet 2[9], 3[7], Acts 20[11–12]). The fact that

man who strives to achieve obedience to God. So earlier E. Schweizer, *Der erste Petrusbrief* (2nd edn, 1949), pp. 54–5; also F. W. Beare, *The First Epistle of Peter* (2nd edn, 1958), pp. 109–10.

A combination of soul and spirit in man, and hence a trichotomy in man's make-up seems to be presupposed in Hebrews 4[12]: 'The Word of God . . . is sharper than a two-edged sword, and pierces through to the dividing of soul and spirit, joints and marrow respectively.' The picture in the writer's mind is here very unclear, but the sentence structure in itself in no way demands a division into soul, spirit, joints and marrow. (This has been suggested by F. Bleek, *Der Brief an die Hebräer*, II.1. [1836].574ff; E. Riggenbach, *Der Brief an die Hebräer* [2nd edn; 3rd edn, 1922], pp. 113–14.) On the contrary, what seems to be envisaged is a time when there will be a dividing of soul from spirit, of joints from marrow—things which are at present inseparably joined. So W. Bauer (note 19, *supra*), p. 999 (ET, pp. 680ff). If this is the case, it is obviously incorrect to conclude that Hebrews advocates a trichotomy in man of body, soul and spirit (Holtzmann [note 9, *supra*], II.328), since *psuche* otherwise in Hebrews denotes the *whole* Christian man and *pneuma* the *divine* Spirit. However, while the dividing of joints from marrow from one another remains a mystery, one cannot go farther than the conclusion that we have here an unemphasized and perhaps unclarified bringing together of two descriptions of the inner man. Cf. E. de Witt Burton (note 3, *supra*), p. 203; E. Schweizer, *ThWb*, VI.444; also C. Spicq, *L'épître aux Hébreux*, II.(1953).89.

man's universal sinfulness cannot be attributed in any way to his material existence is to be set beside the unconditional statement of faith that man like all creation is made by God (1 Pet 4[19], cf. generally Eph 1[4], Heb 1[2, 10], 4[3], 1 Pet 1[20], 2 Pet 3[4–5], Rev 4[11]) and hence is good (1 Tim 4[4]). Men are indeed 'made after the likeness of God' (Jas 3[9], cf. Gen 1[27]). The context of this saying does not help us any further. But the Rabbinic parallels, forbidding the killing of men because man is made in God's image,[96] allow us to suppose that James here thinks of man as the *representation* of God in the world, who in his nature is created after the image of God. The similarity is therefore to be seen in his action and behaviour.[96a]

[96] See references in A. Schlatter, *Der Brief des Jakobus* (1932), p. 228; and J. Marty, *L'épître de Jacques* (1936), p. 135. Cf. *Slavonic Enoch* 44[1], Sect. A (ed. Bonwetsch, p. 41): 'The Lord has with His own hands created men to the likeness of His countenance. . . . He who abuses the countenance of a man, abuses the countenance of a King, and he who abhors the countenance of a man, abhors the countenance of the Lord.'

[96a] Cf. also Eltester (note 78, *supra*), p. 156; Jervell (note 18a, *supra*), p. 240, note 242. J. Héring, *Die biblischen Grundlagen des christlichen Humanismus* (1946), without mentioning James 3[9], urges the thesis that the New Testament teaches 'the real presence of the heavenly Son of Man, the image of God, in every child of man, who is made after His image' (p. 21), from which follows the duty of love for *every* man (Mt 25[40]). Basic to this view should be the assumption that the heavenly Son of Man already in his pre-existence as 'Man' was the image of God, so that 'the empirical man is merely the passing imitation of the eternal heavenly image itself' (p. 11). But this thesis, suggesting a *natural* likeness of man to God through his belonging to the heavenly Archetypal Man, is quite untenable, since according to

Man, however, by the way in which he acts in this world, has reversed his make-up according to God's creation, and, as we have seen, allows himself to be governed by the powers of this world. His love for the world makes him an enemy of God, and this love manifests itself in his subjection to his own lusts (Jas 4^{1-4}, cf. Tit 2^{12}, 3^3). Man here is also seen as a being tied to history within the passing age, who can only be delivered from it by a change in that historical set-up. Thus we may say that there is a homogeneous conception of man in the New Testament underlying all the differences in detail.

There are two exceptions. In the speech of Paul at Areopagus, we find the idea that 'men should seek God for he is not far from each one of us,

'For in Him we live and move and are'; as some of your poets have said: 'We are indeed His offspring.' Being then God's offspring, we ought not to think that God is like gold or silver or stone (Acts 17^{27-9}).

the New Testament view, the image of God does not belong to man's *nature*, but is given to him as a gift. This gift he lost with the Fall into sin, and is first given again through the new creation in Christ (see above, note 78). Apart from that, the Archetypal Man, who would be humbled through his 'incarnation', is not a heavenly 'man' at all, who really shows God's image only in antithesis to the empirical, earthly man. On the contrary, the 'Son of Man' is a heavenly being, who carries the mythical title of 'The Man', without, however, in any way being comparable to *created* man. Despite Héring's denials, there does exist 'an all too familiar equivocation' (p. 10) in the use of the same concept 'The Man' for the Heavenly Man and for earthly man.

Here we see the idea of every man's kinship with God which works itself out within his natural life in God. The other text is 2 Peter 1[4], where the aim of being a Christian is described as: That you may become partakers of the divine nature, having escaped from the transitoriness that is in the world.'[97] It is obvious that in this text the nature of man is described as natural and human, seen as separate from God and manifesting this separation by physical dissolution, which only the gift of a godly nature can cure. Both ideas, that of God's kinship with man, and that of the natural separation of man from God, are completely strange within the context of the other expressions of the New Testament concerning man.[98]

[97] *Phthora* occurs otherwise in 2 Peter 2[12, 19], and only in the sense of 'corruption', 'ruin', so that it is customary to take that meaning also for 1[4]. But in the context, the meaning 'perishableness, transitoriness' is much nearer. This meaning is found in Paul (1 Cor 15[42, 50], Rom 8[21]), and in profane literature (references in Liddell, Scott and Jones, *A Greek-English Lexicon* [1940], p. 1930, No. 2). It is probably preferable, thus translating it here, as above. So also Knopf (note 95, *supra*), pp. 265–6.

[98] The following examples may be named, as illustrating this. For the alleged biblical view 'of a spirit of God in man' only Acts 17[28] can be quoted in the New Testament (C. E. Luthardt, *Kompendium der Dogmatik* [11th edn, 1914], p. 165). And if the Roman Catholic interpretation of the working of justification, '*fit divinae consors naturae*', quotes Patristic support, yet in a great number of such Patristic references the only scriptural support given is 2 Peter 1[4]—apart from the false interpretation of John 1[12–13]. (For Ambrose and Cyril of Alexandria, see M. J. Rouet de Journel, *Enchiridium patristicum* [6th and 7th edns, 1929], Nos. 1283 and 2107, and p. 773.) Martin Werner (*Die Entstehung des christlichen Dogmas* [1941], p. 403) also remarks

But that is only what one would expect from the contexts of both these passages. The idea that man is akin to God is reproduced in Acts 17[28] along with a quotation from the Stoic didactic poem of Aratus, which is introduced by an obviously literary formula. The thought of God's kinship to man is in Acts 17[28] another expression of the fact that man leads his life 'inside' the Godhead. Both ideas, that of the nature and existence of the world and thus of man in God, and that of man's kinship to God are of Stoic origin, and there is nothing to correspond to them in the New Testament.[99] And one cannot get away from this conclusion by diluting this conception of God's existence, interpreting it as 'a pointed reference to the permanent nearness of God', and denuding

upon 2 Peter 1[4] as the single New Testament verse to support the idea of man's becoming as God. G. Didier (*Désintéressement du Chrétien* [1955], p. 231) wrongly quotes also 2 Corinthians 3[18] in support of this idea!

[99] See on this of more recent studies, A. Frövig, '*Das Aratoszitat der Areopagrede des Paulus*', *Symbolae Osloenses* XV–XVI. (1936).44ff; M. Dibelius, '*Paulus auf dem Areopag*', *Aufsätze zur Apostelgeschichte* (2nd edn, 1953), pp. 45ff; M. Pohlenz, '*Paulus und die Stoa*', *ZNW*, XLII.(1949).69ff; H. Hommel, '*Neue Forschungen zur Areopagrede Acta 17*', *ZNW*, XLVI. (1955).145ff, esp. pp. 159, 165ff; H. Hommel, '*Platonisches bei Lukas. Zu Acta 17.28a*', *ZNW*, XLVIII.(1957).193ff; W. Eltester, '*Gott und die Natur in der Areopagrede*', *Neutestamentliche Studien für R. Bultmann* (2nd edn, 1957), pp. 202ff; E. Haenchen, *Die Apostelgeschichte* (12th edn, 1959), pp. 453ff; H. Conzelmann, '*Die Rede des Paulus auf dem Areopag*', *Gymnasium Helveticum*, XII.(1958).18ff; E. Grässer, '*Die Apostelgeschichte in der Forschung der Gegenwart*', *ThR*, XXVI.(1960). 140ff.

the quotation from Aratus of its Hellenistic sense
by talking of the biblical basis of the speech.[100]
It is only natural that the Areopagus speech should
contain a Hellenistic understanding of man in
relation to God. For the Areopagus speech is, as
M. Dibelius has conclusively shown,[101] 'a hellen-

[100] So O. Bauernfeind, *Die Apostelgeschichte* (1939), p. 219;
but also similarly H. W. Beyer, *Die Apostelgeschichte* (1932),
p. 104. Hanson ([note 72, *supra*], pp. 102–3) understands *en auto*
as analogous to *en Christo*, meaning belonging together with God
to a living *corpus*, and *theou genos* as meaning belonging 'to the
great *corpus* of humanity which God created, and whose Head
and Lord is God Himself'. But this exegesis is a pure postulate
on the basis of the Creation thought found in Acts 17²⁴⁻⁶. Again,
one cannot simply dismiss the opposition to Paul here by referring to 'other teaching of Paul', as does N. B. Stonehouse (*Paul
before the Areopagus* [1957], p. 29). Nor can one ignore the
thought of the relationship of man to God, by regarding 17²⁸ on
the basis of its connexion with 17²⁹ as merely an attack on the
service of idols, and the thought 'in Him we live and move and
have our being' as simply an expression of 'man's absolute
dependence on God' (so B. Gärtner, *The Areopagus Speech and
Natural Revelation* [1955], pp. 164ff, 178ff). H. P. Owen ('The
Scope of Natural Revelation in Romans 1 and Acts 17', *NTSt*,
V.[1958/9], pp. 133ff) explains quite uncritically Acts 17²⁷⁻⁸ on
the basis of Romans 1¹⁸ff. The translation '*through* whom we live
. . .' suggested by him and by G. Lindeskog ([note 72, *supra*],
p. 190) is hardly possible in this context, formed as it is in
Hellenistic terms. On the other hand, W. Nauck (in '*Die Tradition und Komposition der Areopagrede*', *ZThK*, LIII.[1956].
11ff, esp. pp. 22, 43ff), who believes that a real sermon of Paul's
in Athens lies behind the Areopagus speech, expressly excludes
from this supposed Pauline draft all mention of the Hellenistic
thought of the divinization of man.

[101] Note 99, *supra*. Dibelius has sought to demonstrate this
thesis not only through comparisons of a history-of-religions
kind between the particular groups of ideas of the Areopagus
speech and the biblical material, but also by suggesting a new

istic speech concerning the true knowledge of God',
which stands alone within the New Testament in
its whole tone and in many of its expressions, and
which can only be seen as the precursor of the
philosophical theology of the second-century Apol-
ogists. The stoic-pantheistic understanding of man

'philosophical' meaning for the 'seasons' and 'territories' given
to man of Acts 17^{26}, which, in spite of some difficulties, has great
probability in favour of it. Cf. recently Haenchen (note 99,
supra), ad. loc. W. Schmid (*Die Rede des Apostels Paulus vor den
Philosophen und Areopagisten in Athen*', *Philologus*, XCV.[1942].
79ff) not only rejects this new meaning for Acts 17^{26}, but also
attempts to prove the 'historicity' of the Areopagus speech and
also the consistency of its thought with Paul throughout. Schmid
believes himself to establish what Paul must have said to the
philosophers in the spiritual situation of the Athens of that day,
what larger connexions of thought the fragments of Acts 17^{22ff}
must have formed part of, and finally what thoughts of the
original speech must have been lost in the tradition. By this
highly questionable method, it is then established that the
quotation from Aratos could only have meant for Paul 'that
idolatry was also rejected by Greeks' (p. 106), and that 'the
hellenistic views in the Areopagus speech . . . were not appro-
priated by Paul, but were brought in as witnesses against idolatry
from the Greek side' (p. 111, note 100); important leading
pieces of the original speech would have been allowed to be lost
in the repeating of the story in Acts 17^{22ff}. These are, however,
quite untenable assertions, which completely ignore the purpose
of the author in including this speech in his work. (Page 113,
note 113, regards the concluding appeal to *metanoia* in 17^{30} as
unsuitable for the historical situation, but then attributes it to
the passionate zeal of the apostle, while at the same time it is
rightly pointed out that the appeal for conversion 'regularly
concludes the mission sermons of Acts'!) Schmid does not
mention that the Areopagus speech is unique in the whole New
Testament, so that the thesis of Dibelius does not appear in any
way to be superseded by these considerations. R. Liechtenhan
(*Die urchristliche Mission* [1946], pp. 92ff) agrees with Dibelius

in Acts 17^{28} cannot be brought into harmony with the rest of the New Testament.[101a]

Again, when 2 Peter 1^4 describes the aim of redemption as flight from transitoriness and participation in the divine *phusis*, and conceives man's nature as being *inherently* shut out from God, then we must conclude that that also is a definite expression of the Hellenistic view of man, which

that the speech in its present form is Hellenistic, and thus could not have been given by Paul, but wishes to insist that 'there are yet elements in its contents which belonged to the Gentile mission preaching of Paul'. Liechtenhan argues that the speech only gives a fragment of the sermon, which Paul intended to give, he being prevented from concluding it. The latter is an assertion which attributes to the author of Acts a far too exact observation of what might have been possible in the special situation in Athens. No one would wish to deny that the Areopagus speech contains thoughts which actually belonged to the mission preaching of Paul—as, for instance, the polemic against image-worship, mentioned by Liechtenhan. But the decisive question is whether the leading concepts of the speech are in agreement with Pauline theology. And this, it must be admitted, certainly cannot be said for the ideas in 17$^{28-9}$. Against B. Gärtner's attempt to prove the whole speech as Pauline, cf. Grässer (note 99, *supra*), pp. 140ff. It cannot therefore be doubted that the thesis of Dibelius has correctly given the historical circumstances.

[101a] When Hebrews 2^{11} says that 'he who consecrates and those whom he consecrates are all of one', the *henos*, 'of one', doubtless is to be related to God—so recently Spicq (note 95, *supra*), p. 41. But that does not imply the common affinity with God of both Saviour and those saved, as E. Käsemann (*Das wandernde Gottesvolk* [1938 = 3rd edn, 1959], pp. 90–1) suggests. The reference is to God as Creator. Cf. H. Windisch, *Der Hebräerbrief* (2nd edn, 1931), p. 22; O. Michel, *Der Brief an die Hebräer* (8th edn, 1949), p. 80; Lindeskog (note 72, *supra*), p. 185.

presupposes the dualism between the earthly, material world and the divine, spiritual world.[102] This is, in fact, what would be expected, for 2 Peter, in spite of his retention of the early Christian expectation of the coming judgement, also sets beside it a timeless Hellenistic view of salvation, which does not fit in with the historical idea of salvation in the New Testament.[103] There can therefore be no question that both texts, Acts 17[28] and 2 Peter 1[4], imply anthropological ideas which do not accord with the picture of man in the rest of the New Testament.[104] This, however, is not astonishing, for both texts in their contexts and their whole theological bearing belong only to the fringe of the New Testament.

All the same, we must conclude that it is not permissible to put every statement in the New Testament about man on the same level. If one is to combine the concepts of man in Acts 17[28] and 2 Peter 1[4] with the expressions used elsewhere in the New Testament, one must simply either be content with this contradictory and divisive picture or else spoil the otherwise uniform picture of man in the New Testament by giving equal weight to these two texts, which, in any case, do not agree

[102] See the references in Knopf (note 95, *supra*), pp. 264–5.

[103] For proof, see Windisch (note 95, *supra*), p. 85.

[104] So also Lindeskog (note 72, *supra*), p. 190. Confirmation of the remark above can be found in the fact that the word '*theios*', so characteristic of Hellenistic thought, only occurs twice in the New Testament, in Acts 17[29] and 2 Peter 1[3–4]. Cf. H. Kleinknecht, *ThWb*, III.123.

with one another. The only other possibility would
be to reinterpret these two texts in the light of all
the other texts, which would indeed be absurd.
Rather must we take the fact of the canon seriously
as a *historical* norm, whose rightness and validity
must always be open to scholarly investigation.
An uncritical biblicism, which excludes such investigation, is so much concerned to preserve an
apparent unit of the *whole* New Testament, that
the singular character of the New Testament revelation is endangered by making it conform to the
world-view of its day. Consequently, the distinction between the central biblical concepts and the
extra-biblical ideas is obliterated. One of the most
important tasks, as yet unattempted, of a New
Testament scholarship which is consciously biblical yet critically honest, is that of showing where
in the New Testament there are '*borders*' which
can be found by taking into account particular
concepts and circles of thought. By 'borders' I
mean concepts which are actually to be found
within the New Testament but which cannot be
brought into real consistency with the rest of the
New Testament. Such a task would constitute a
singular contribution to an understanding of the
central message of the New Testament.[105]

[105] I have attempted to develop the corresponding proof with
regard to the New Testament concept of Faith in the article,
'*Der Glaube im Neuen Testament, seine katholische und reforma-
torische Deutung*', *ThBl*, XVI.(1937).209ff. Cf. also on the
intrusion of foreign motives in New Testament Ethics, Preisker
(note 81, *supra*), pp. 195ff; and the remarks on legendary

In spite of the fact that we must conclude on exegetical grounds that the two texts Acts 17^{28} and 2 Peter 1^4 appear as strange within the New Testament picture of man, and are to be attributed to the intrusion of Hellenistic ideas, yet the rest of the New Testament presents us with a unified picture. And this confronts us all today with the question whether or not we want to recognize the New Testament's picture of ourselves. Once we have recognized that this picture was formulated solely upon the basis of the new creation which resulted from God's action in Christ, *as it was experienced in the life of men*, then we cannot avoid the conclusion that we *must* recognize this picture of man as correct, if we also have ourselves affirmed personally such a belief in the saving act of God in Christ. The historical picture of man in the New Testament is one which is conditioned by Christian faith, and therefore cannot be expected to commend itself to a non-Christian world. But just because every man does not naturally think of himself as the New Testament supposes

inroads in the Canon and on the inconstant borders of the Canon in the Gospels and Acts, by K. L. Schmidt, *Kanonische und apokryphe Evangelien und Apostelgeschichten* (1944), pp. 22–3. On the theological problem of the borders of the Canon, cf. recently H. Strathmann, '*Die Krisis des Kanons der Kirche*', *ThBl*, XX.(1941).295ff; E. Brunner, *Offenbarung und Vernunft* (1941), pp. 129ff; W. G. Kümmel, '*Notwendigkeit und Grenze des neutestamentlichen Kanons*', *ZThK*, XLVII.(1950).277ff; O. Weber, *Grundlagen der Dogmatik*, I.(1955).274ff; H. Braun, '*Hebt die neutestamentlich-exegetische Forschung den Kanon auf?*' *Fuldaer Hefte*, XII.(1960).9ff.

him to do, this does not mean that the Christian understanding of him is not the one which describes him as he really is.

Index
of New Testament Texts